*Prussians in the Place
de la Concorde*

Paris under Siege

A journal of the events of
1870-1871
kept by contemporaries and translated
and presented by
Joanna Richardson

London
The Folio Society
1982

Set in eleven point Ehrhardt type leaded two points
and printed by Western Printing Services Ltd, Bristol
on Guard Bridge Fine Book Laid paper.
Illustrations printed by Jolly & Barber Ltd, Rugby.
Bound by The Pitman Press Ltd, Bath
in Wicotex Relay book cloth
printed lithographically.

Printed in Great Britain

Contents

List of Illustrations

*Except where otherwise stated, all the illustrations are taken from
Stephen Holder's collection and photographed by John Freeman & Co.
The Folio Society would like to thank Stephen Holder for his invaluable
help and advice.*

Preface

This is not a political or military history. It is not a detailed narrative of the Franco-Prussian War, of the Siege of Paris and the Commune. It is something which, I think, has not yet been attempted: a contemporary journal of events in Paris from the fall of the Second Empire on 4 September 1870, to the fall of the Commune on 28 May 1871.

L'année terrible began with the declaration of the Franco-Prussian War: a catastrophic war which France declared without any valid reason, and without preparation. Bellicose and ill-equipped, led by an ailing Emperor, an incompetent Government, and by generals who were past their prime, she chose to go to war with Prussia. She was determined to contest the supremacy of Prussian arms in Europe, the prospect of a united Germany. Seven weeks later, after a series of heavy defeats, the Emperor surrendered and the Second Empire fell.

The Republic was proclaimed, but the war continued. The most disastrous months were yet to come. The Prussians laid siege to Paris. The Parisians faced the siege with complex emotions: terror and insouciance, indecision and heroism. Some Parisians were practical; all too many of them showed their habitual sense of theatre. General Trochu, the Governor of Paris, Commander-in-Chief of the Armée de Paris, recognized the Prussians' superiority when he explained: 'They have no time for gold lace or demonstrations, they sacrifice everything to the effectiveness of the enterprise.'

It was apparent from the first that unless the Parisian forces made a victorious assault on the enemy, unless a provincial army rescued it, Paris would finally have to surrender. In fact the great sortie was not made, and no relieving army ever came. Paris was heroic, but it was impractical. It was bombarded, needlessly starved into submission. 'The Parisians', wrote an English observer, 'find it impossible to understand that the world at large can see little distinction between a French army entering Berlin and a Prussian army entering Paris. Their capital is to them a holy city.' Holy it remained; but, on 1 March 1871, the Prussians made their triumphal entry down the Champs-Élysées.

Peace was signed, and it was shameful. Subsequent events were more shameful still. The Commune seized power in Paris, and French troops were obliged to begin a second, far more bitter siege of the city. Some members of the Commune were extreme Republicans, some of them were merely anarchists. They drew to themselves all the disaffected and violent in Paris. Many people 'who were gentle, docile, and good workers, were disturbed by new thoughts when the Commune came; extraordinary hopes awoke in them, unknown perspectives opened to their wondering eyes. The Commune was the day of the people which was dawning, the reign of the working man which had begun.' The Commune brought no democracy or republican Utopia. It brought destruction, violence and hatred. As Maxime du Camp explained in *Les Convulsions de Paris*,

the whole menagerie of bad passions broke out of its cage during the Commune, and, for two long months, it revelled in utter bestiality in the midst of the most extreme moral collapse that history had ever recorded. One cannot reproach the Commune for being hypocritical; it did not disguise itself in the least; it was very honest. Like a shameless prostitute, it showed everything, and people were surprised by the dreadful ulcers which corroded it. What it was then, it would be again, because it is the product of the human vice *par excellence*, the vice of envy.

After the war, the Sacré-Coeur was built at Montmartre, where the Commune had begun; it was built, by public subscription, to atone for the events of *l'année terrible*, and to ask God's forgiveness and protection for Paris. Vast, Byzantine, alien, it does not compensate for the French destruction of Saint-Cloud, or for the burning of the Tuileries.

Here are the events of nine unforgotten months, from September 1870 to May 1871. They are recorded by those who witnessed them. Some – like Queen Victoria – saw them in international perspective. Some – like Flaubert – watched them, helplessly, from the provinces. The Crown Prince of Prussia, Field-Marshal Count von Moltke, and the anonymous officer in the Prussian Garde Landwehr, recorded the impressions of besiegers. Most of the comments were made by people living in Paris. Their immediacy is more poignant, more significant than any twentieth-century account. As far as possible, I have left them to write the narrative.

I must express my thanks to the staff of the British Library, for their patient help. I should also like to record my gratitude to King's College, London, and especially to Mr H. A. Harvey, for allowing me to use the diary and letters of Edwin Child.

JOANNA RICHARDSON
August 1979

Introduction

Early in July 1870, Count Bismarck advanced a Hohenzollern candidate, Prince Leopold of Sigmaringen, to fill the vacant throne of Spain. France expressed such violent alarm at this threatened act of 'encirclement' that the candidate was promptly withdrawn. But France needed war. Ever since 1866, when Prussia defeated Austria at Sadowa, France had been aware of the Prussian challenge to her grandeur. No French Government could idly watch while Prussia united Germany under her, and the Press began to stir up warlike feeling. The Emperor was sixty-two, and in lamentable health; he had no wish for war. Nor had Émile Ollivier, who had recently come to power. But the Emperor was being pushed by his foreign minister, the Duc de Gramont (who was still smarting from Bismarck's comment: 'The stupidest man in Europe'); he was also being pushed towards war by the Empress, who declared that their son would not reign unless they retrieved the misfortune of Sadowa.

Gramont now assumed a hectoring tone towards Prussia. It was not enough that she had withdrawn her candidate, she must be humbled for her presumption. He therefore cabled Count Benedetti, the Ambassador in Berlin, to keep the crisis hot. William I of Prussia, who was taking the waters at Ems, received Benedetti on 13 July with the greatest courtesy, and assured him that no one wanted war less than he did. He considered the unification of Germany his grandson's task, not his own. But while the Emperor was being pushed by Gramont, the King was being pushed by Bismarck. On his momentous visit to Paris in 1867, Bismarck had observed that the French army was pitiably unprepared for modern warfare; and he had diligently trained a massive, modern army of his own. He had long since decided that war with France would cement the German federation.

The pretext had to be carefully chosen, for it had to be one that showed France in the most unfavourable light. Now that France was insisting on further diplomatic victories, trying to humble Prussian pride, and showing quite unnecessary belligerence, Bismarck decided that the time had come. At Ems, the King had been irritated by Benedetti's insistence on a guarantee that the Hohenzollern candidature would not arise again. He declined to give such a guarantee, and refused Benedetti's request for a further audience. A telegram describing his refusal was despatched to Bismarck in Berlin. Bismarck sharpened the tone, and stated that the King had 'refused to receive the Ambassador again, and he had had the latter informed by the adjutant on duty that His Majesty had no further communication to make.' Bismarck sent his version of the Ems Telegram to the Berlin Press and to every capital in Europe.

Even with Bismarck's editing, the Ems Telegram was hardly a *casus belli*; but it was enough to entice Napoleon III into the trap.

On Friday, 15 July, the Minister for Foreign Affairs gave the Senate the official account of the talks at Ems between the King of Prussia and Benedetti. 'We have done everything', he said, 'to avoid a war, we shall prepare to fight the war which is offered to us.'

At half-past nine that night the Emperor presided over a council of ministers at Saint-Cloud. At midnight the ministers left the palace. 'It is war!' declared *Le Moniteur universel*. 'God save France!'

On 28 July the Emperor and the Prince Imperial, a boy of fourteen, left Saint-Cloud to join the Rhine Army headquarters at Metz.

No well-informed Frenchman could have wanted war with Prussia, for the French army was quite unprepared. But the disorderly regiments entrained for the frontier. The Empress had urged her husband to assume command of the armies, so that MacMahon would take orders from him. Her arrogance and stupidity seemed almost beyond belief. Napoleon III had only book knowledge and the brief Italian campaign behind him. He was being urged to command a Marshal of France. He was in such pain from gallstones that he could hardly sit his horse; he was being forced to direct a campaign which needed the tactical genius of the great Napoleon in his prime.

Within two days of the Emperor's arrival at Metz, Eugénie had a letter in which he told her of the confusion and chaos, the lack of co-ordination and supplies. The first necessity of his strategy was to launch an attack across the Rhine – but now an attack was out of the question. On 2 August he announced a slight advance at Saarbrücken. On 6 August the armies of MacMahon and Frossard were beaten at Forbach and Froeschwiller. Soon after ten o'clock that night a tele-gram arrived at Saint-Cloud. It began: 'Our troops are in full retreat. Nothing must be thought of now except the defence of the capital.'

The preparations for the Fête Napoléon – an annual public holiday – were cancelled, and the great imperial crown, hoisted to the top of the Arc de Triomphe, was brought down. On 21 August Felix White-hurst, the *Daily Telegraph* correspondent in Paris, declared that 'as for investing Paris, that is absurd: it would take a million of men. There are thirty-two miles of fortifications.'* Yet with every day the siege came nearer. On 29 August he observed that all the streets were 'crowded with furniture waggons – coming from and going to stations – and country carts. Every family that has any family place goes to it, while all the small proprietors and little farmers near Paris are coming in to the shelter of the guns and the city barricades . . . Food is already 25% dearer.'† By 30 August the butchers were refusing credit. No morning mail left Paris that day. Prussian troops were within a few hours of the capital.

On Saturday, 3 September, the news reached Paris. The Emperor, debilitated by gallstones and prostate trouble, worn by the fatigues and trials of the campaign, had surrendered with his army at Sedan. A French correspondent of *The Times* confessed: 'Our worst fears fell short of this. I must leave to your English correspondents the task of comment; I feel unequal to it. God help poor France!'‡

The Emperor a prisoner [Whitehurst wrote next day]! Eighty thou-sand prisoners, and 200 guns lost! . . .

The evil news soon leaked out yesterday . . .

As soon as day of Sunday, 4 September, dawned, Paris, or at least a large section of it, arose mad with republican excitement . . .

At 12 o'clock you could not thrust your way down the rue de Rivoli . . .

Of course every shop was closed, and the shopkeeper with his wife (if he was too old for active service) sitting on chairs out on the pavement . . . The imperial standard was still hanging listlessly over the Court of Honour of the Tuileries, as if it guessed that its last wave was at hand.*

That day, the fall of the Empire and the Bonaparte dynasty was decreed, and the French Republic was proclaimed. At half-past three the imperial standard was finally hauled down from the Pavillon de l'Horloge, at the Tuileries. The Empress was smuggled out of Paris by her American dentist.

Next day, on the gates of the Tuileries facing the place de la Concorde, passers-by saw two wreaths of immortelles. They re-affirmed the death of the Second Empire.†

Part One

Preparation

Napoleon III and the Prince Imperial leaving to join the Rhine Army

Napoleon III enters the Prussian camp after the Battle of Sedan

SEPTEMBER 1870

The Napoleonic years had ended, and Paris greeted the news with jubilation. The imperial eagles were torn down from Garnier's new Opéra; and the populace swarmed up the grand staircase at the Tuileries, and into the Salle des Maréchaux, and scrawled graffiti on the palace walls.

The Emperor was imprisoned at Wilhelmshohe, in what was soon to be the German Empire. The Empress and her son had escaped to England, Princess Mathilde to Belgium, Prince Napoleon to Italy. There was a flood of virulent anti-Bonaparte cartoons, of scurrilous anti-Bonaparte pamphlets. The crown diamonds had been hidden in the naval arsenal at Brest, but they were eventually to be auctioned. Such was the bitterness in politics that even the Emperor's foreign decorations were to be broken up and destroyed. France could not do enough to show her hatred and contempt for Napoléon le Petit. The republic began with a violence which had not been known since the French Revolution.

Paris was so intent on destroying the final vestiges of the Second Empire that, for a moment, the Prussian invaders were forgotten. But the Emperor's defeat had not brought the end of the Franco-Prussian War, and the enemy were still marching on Paris. By 8 September nine out of every ten Parisians were in uniform, and squads were drilling in the streets from six o'clock in the morning.

There were crowds in the open air as ever [reported John Augustus O'Shea, the Paris correspondent of the *Standard*]. The thoroughfares blossomed with uniforms; the omnibuses, which plied as usual, were crowded with freights of soldiery; even the few passers-by in paletot generally had a red stripe on their trousers to show or hint that they belonged to the National Guard. The females reduced their chignons and went about in modest, pensive grey or black. One day I met Blanche Pierson, the pretty actress of the Gymnase. She had laid aside her sheeny satins and full flounces, and was hardly to be recognised . . . It was correct to be matronly.*

American women who had come to Paris to patronize Worth, to carry home some prestigious sample of *haute couture*, seemed likely to be foiled by events.

The railroads were so overworked [recorded Wickham Hoffman, the Secretary at the American Legation], that they finally refused to take any baggage that could not be carried by the passenger himself. Imagine the painful situation of some of our fair countrywomen, Worth's admirers and patrons! To have come to Paris amidst all the dangers of war to procure something to wear, to have procured it, and then to be unable to carry it away! But what will not woman's wit and energy do under such circumstances? A clever and energetic friend of mine hired a *bateau-mouche*, one of the little steamers that ply on the Seine from one part of Paris to another, and, embarking with her *impedimenta*, sailed triumphantly from Le Havre.*

Many visitors were leaving Paris. Many who lived in the suburbs were coming in to seek the safety of the fortifications. Mrs Griffin, an American resident, recorded them in *Pictures from Paris. In War and in Siege*.

Beyond the Arc de Triomphe, amid the Bois de Boulogne, and the plain of Longchamp, what do we see? Also on the long road of the Elysian Fields, and on the diverging highways to the west, south, and north? Carriages, vans, carts, waggons, wheelbarrows, trays on wheels, all laden with household goods, and accompanied by their now houseless owners, weary and depressed, seeking asylum in Paris ...

Long Normandy carts, drawn by awkward broad-backed farm horses 'dragged their slow length along', and as we looked at the human freight packed together with beds, bedding, chairs, tables, faded tapestry, bird-cages, and pet dogs, we could not refrain from tears; and when some aged woman would meet our view, perched at a dangerous height on a pile of mattresses, and surrounded by her children and grandchildren walking in melancholy procession in the dust of the wheels, never perhaps to return to the old home, we were deeply, deeply pained. Thus they swarmed into Paris – Paris, the dragon that devours the nation.

We not only met the poor, but every now and then a private carriage, with a coronet on its polished panels, with closed windows and drawn blinds, but protruding from the half-open doors were rare old china monsters, and we caught a hasty glimpse of ormolu, statuettes, bronzes, cabinet-pictures, and ornate time-pieces. Cabs bore pyramids of bonnet-boxes and trunks; barouches dashed by with dressing-cases and gilt cages; there followed lumbering vans, and in fact every conceivable shape of vehicle.*

A French observer, Édouard Cabrol, continued:

Crowds of terrified provincials were arriving by train in Paris . . .

In our railway stations, in Paris, bundles, baggages and furniture lay scattered even along the track. People were looking for their belongings in an indescribable confusion. The porters had given up distributing these things to their owners . . .

Many orderly people had wanted to bring everything. Goats were wandering between the rails . . . Sometimes a diabolical din came out of a tied-up basket. Its inhabitant was trying to escape; some cat or poodle had started to die of hunger. Here and there, in the tunnels, on the platforms, everywhere, there were upturned cages, sometimes upside-down, where philosophical canaries were whistling their little tune, half-stifled under the corner of a mattress . . .

In the streets, there was nothing but refugees, who hadn't washed for two days, and were looking for lodgings so that they could install a wash-stand . . .

It was just a premature rout, a sign of the general disarray . . .

In fact, in every class of society, there was terror; and nothing, for the moment, could prevail against it.†

O'Shea took a less emotional view of the situation. 'It is', he wrote, 'an axiom of war that a besieged stronghold must surrender if the besieger has adequate resources at his command, unless a relieving army smashes up the attack. Time is on the side of the besieger.' The siege of Paris was 'a Titanic undertaking – the greatest siege the world had ever witnessed; but the Germans remembered that . . . Paris was in a wretched state of unpreparedness.' Yet O'Shea was not wholly pessimistic. 'The case of Paris was by no means hopeless, had the proper man been in sole authority, and had he the proper material to mould into shape.'*

The Governor of Paris, the Commander-in-Chief of the Armée de Paris, was General Louis-Jules Trochu. He was fifty-five, and he had had a remarkably distinguished career in Algeria, the Crimea, and Italy. His career might have been more distinguished still had he been a man of ambition, and had he not earned the fear and intense dislike of the Empress. In 1867 he had published a tract called *L'Armée Française*; he had all too accurately shown the weaknesses of the French army, and pointed out the failings of the Government.

In August 1870, after the outbreak of the Franco-Prussian War, he had addressed a letter to the Emperor's War Council, and in it he had already spoken of a siege of Paris. 'The essential condition of a siege, imperatively necessary for this one, is that the struggle should be supported by a relieving army . . . to act by repeated attacks against the Prussian Army, which would as a consequence be incapable of a complete investment.' Within a few days of writing this letter he had been appointed Governor of Paris, and he had been entrusted with its defence. On 25 August he had complained that, since he assumed his post, he had 'received from the Government neither verbally nor in writing, neither directly nor indirectly, neither in confidence nor otherwise, any communication whatsoever relative to the movement of the Prussian Army. The defence of Paris is reduced . . . to the rumours of the newspapers.'† He discharged his duties, so it seems, with alternate moods of vigour and lethargy, purposeful action and withdrawal from responsibility.

On 8 September Jules Claretie, the chronicler and man of letters, called on Trochu.

General Trochu received me in a charming manner, like a man of the world and like a soldier . . . I immediately felt the charm which this pleasant talker, this irresolute soldier – we have since learned this lesson – can give to the turn of a conversation. He charmed me, and he saddened me; his hopes had had their wings terribly torn by the recent defeats.

'If I had a relieving army,' he said to me, 'I could conquer. I should defend the environs of Paris. I should defend all those villages which won't serve me as outposts, but will serve as shelter to the besiegers. Oh, if I had MacMahon's hundred and twenty thousand men round Paris! But what is Vinoy's army? We are at the Prussians' disposal. If they want to make a sudden attack, with their artillery, they will take a fort, two forts, three forts, Issy, Vanves, Montrouge; they'll bombard the faubourg Saint-Germain, they'll start fires here and there . . . But we must still save our honour and the Republic, for I think that monarchy in any form, constitutional or authoritarian, is finished! But our adversaries are such practical people. They have no time for gold lace or demonstrations, they sacrifice everything to the effectiveness of the enterprise!' And he repeated: 'If only I had a relieving army!'*

Victor Hugo, now sixty-eight, had returned from his self-imposed exile the moment that the Empire had fallen. He issued a pontifical declaration: 'Germans, if you persist, so be it. You have been warned. Now come! Come and attack the walls of Paris. Under your bombs and your mitrailleuses she will defend herself. As for me – an old man, now – I shall be there unarmed. It behoves me to be with the people who die. I pity you for being with the kings who kill.'†

On 9 September, from Neuilly, Théophile Gautier, the poet, wrote to his daughter Estelle in Switzerland. He had chosen to leave the security of Geneva, the company of Carlotta Grisi – who remained the love of his life – and to come home to share the fate of Paris.

My dear Estelle,

. . . I arrived this morning with a train of militia; we were afraid the train might be intercepted at any moment, but we passed through without any trouble . . . Paris is very strange just now. All along the route there are soldiers, front-line troops, militia and others, sleeping in tents and cooking in the open air. It is pouring torrents, which will delay the Prussians a little; they will be in Paris at the beginning of next week . . . They're demolishing the houses and felling the trees in the outer zone, and the ruins look lugubrious in the rain . . . We haven't yet left Neuilly where I found the aunts better and more settled. Don't worry at all about our fate. We have enough money to live on for at least two months even if they didn't print a single line of copy. The affair of the *Officiel* may perhaps be arranged . . . The railways will no doubt be cut tomorrow or some time later, and if you don't receive letters regularly and even if you don't receive any at all you mustn't be alarmed on that account . . .

Your father,

THÉOPHILE GAUTIER*

Two days later he wrote to Carlotta:

You know already that I arrived safely in Paris. They're preparing for a desperate defence. We are still at Neuilly. When it is time to fall back on the capital, the mayor will proclaim it by beat of drums, and we shall all go in together, escorted by the Garde nationale. I am still at *Le Journal Officiel*. I have enough to live on for six weeks or two months, and, unless a shell falls right on my head, I am as safe as anyone can be at such a time. We are going to live at 12, rue de Beaune, near the paper, and that is where you must write to us from now on. You can't imagine what Paris looks like, especially the suburbs, for towards the centre you are less aware of the situation we are in. From the Arc de Triomphe to the bridge, the avenue de Neuilly is one enormous military camp with troops from every branch of the service: troops of the line, cavalry, artillery, cannon, machine-guns, ammunition-waggons. The Tuileries gardens, which are closed, have become a great park full of soldiers, horses and cannon. Over the pavillon de l'Horloge, where the tricolour flag used to fly, there floats the Swiss flag with the red cross on a white ground, because they have turned the palace into a field-hospital. They have re-opened closed cemeteries to bury the dead who will not fail to come. We are living in a nightmare and one's spirit refuses to believe that everything is real. In two or three days, the enemy will be outside Paris . . . A fixed battle is impossible. The war of the partisans is going to begin. Yesterday they burned the houses in the Bicêtre region – the inhabitants didn't know where to go, and didn't want to move. Half of the Bois de Boulogne has been felled. The pont de Neuilly has been mined and it will blow up some morning or other. In two or three days they will set fire to the woods of Meudon, Ville d'Avray and Bondy, and to all the crops which still remain standing. There is nothing so sad as these processions of waggons, carts, hand-carts, wheelbarrows, cabs, which are verging on Paris bringing pathetic furniture with women and children sitting on mattresses. You would think that they were escaping from a flood which nothing can prevent.*

On 12 September Juliette Adam, wife of Edmond Adam, the journalist and politician, recorded:

I'm trotting about all over the place getting my provisions; I need so many things! Anything can be lacking at any moment, even salt and pepper and mustard. I'm showing all my domestic genius in my research. I dream of nothing but Australian mutton, Liebig ham, Chollet vegetables, groceries and victuals. My pockets and dress and arms and hands are always chock-full when I come home. If I find a new preserve, I imagine the surprise it's going to give in three months' time to the friends I invite to eat it! If I see heroes spring up around me, I shan't weave wreaths for them, or deck their houses with garlands, I shall offer them a jar of new preserved carrots.†

The heroes were yet to show themselves; but, on 14 September,

General Trochu issued an order of the day to the Gardes nationaux of the Seine, and the Gardes mobiles.

Never has any general witnessed the great spectacle that you afford me: three hundred battalions of citizens, organized and armed, surrounded by the entire population, acclaiming in vast concert the defence of Paris and of freedom...

With our formidable effective force, the daily guard in Paris will never be less than 70,000 men. If the enemy pierced the enceinte by storm, or by surprise, or by an open breach, he would meet the barricades which are now being built, and the leaders of the enemy columns would then be defeated by the attack of ten echelons of reserves.

Have complete faith, then, and know that the enceinte of Paris, defended by the persevering effort of public spirit and by three hundred thousand rifles, is unapproachable.

Gardes nationaux of the Seine and Gardes mobiles,

In the name of the Government of National Defence, of which I am only the representative, I thank you for your patriotic concern for the cherished interests which are entrusted to you.

And now, to work in the nine sections of the defences! Let there be order, calm, devotion everywhere! And remember, as I have already told you, that you remain in charge of the policing of Paris in these days of crisis.

Prepare to suffer with fortitude. If you do so, you will conquer.*

The plague is coming near [continued Mme Adam, the same day]; the enemy is approaching Paris; the Prussian invasion is flooding, unimpeded, over our old Champagne, whose plains have seen so many heroic fights. The courage of the people of Paris grows greater every hour. Crowds of workmen, at our gates, are digging trenches and building ramparts. On the boulevards, all day and all night, I hear the shells and bullets as they pass, rattling, knocking together, and echoing with a sinister sound in the ordnance carts...†

Next morning, 15 September, recorded Major William Blumé, of the Prussian Ministry of War, 'orders for the investment of Paris were issued from Headquarters . . . The object was to isolate the place completely, and to defeat all attempts to supply or relieve it.'*

How long shall we be besieged like this [asked an anonymous Parisian]?

I don't know; but, alas! I am obliged to say this, because I have sworn to speak the truth: I don't believe in a very long resistance.

We have no discipline.

Our cannon are still at Sedan.

Our soldiers are prisoners, and the new army is made up of citizens who are ignorant of military matters; all its weapons are useless.

Determination means strength, they say. Alas! Shall we have the determination?†

Ernest Renan showed determination. That day he assured a correspondent: 'I shan't leave Paris for a single moment. I have sent my children to Brittany; but my wife and I will stay, whatever happens. I believe that it is a duty, in such circumstances, to show that one is present; and, completely powerless as one is, to keep what little strength one possesses at the service of reason and of one's native land.‡

Felix Whitehurst:
                                                           17 September
By the time we get a little picrate of potash and a few bombs and shells, Paris will be, as Moore said of Ireland, 'a charming place to live out of.' It is now mined all round, and within it is one depôt of petroleum . . .

I have just returned from the Tower of Solferino, a monument erected close to the Place de Saint-Pierre . . . It was a lovely cloudless day, and the whole city . . . glittered in the sun. The sailors worked gaily at a fort; a long line of white tents glistened on the heights to our right; bugles were sounding, drums beating, and soldiers parading everywhere, while a large idle crowd formed a hedge around

M. Nadar and his captive balloon. And yet the scene was depressing to an extreme degree. In whichever direction you turned your glass, you saw signs of the rapid advance of war – villages deserted, houses pulled down; the wretched inhabitants pouring into Paris, and last, but not least, wood after wood from Paris to Pierrefitte smouldering away in deep smoke or burning briskly in the keen north wind.*

Edmond de Goncourt:

17 September

In Boulogne [in the south-west suburbs of Paris], all the blinds drawn in the windows, all the shutters closed in the shops. There is nothing open, now, except the pork-butcher, the wine-merchant, the hair-dresser. In the deserted village, a few removal carts, parked without horses, are standing in front of mattresses and bed-linen, which have been thrown down on the pavement. Here and there a few old women sit in the sun in front of some obscure alleyway, stubbornly staying and wanting to die where they have spent their lives.

In the narrow cross streets, lifeless and deserted, pigeons walk and hop about on the pavement, where no living creature disturbs them.†

On 18 September, waiting at Corbeil, Field-Marshal Count von Blumenthal recorded:

No news tonight. It looks as if the arrangements for the investment of the town were going along quietly. Tomorrow the chain will be complete, and then nobody will be able to come out of nor go into Paris.

The French have up to date made no attempt at treating, and I am very curious to know how it will end. We may perhaps have to sit down for weeks before Paris. The way things have been destroyed is too childish. Here, for instance, the piles of a bridge have been blown up, and thereby a large number of houses damaged.

We were not delayed by it, however, for the Bavarian Pontoon Section came up and built a bridge in the twinkling of an eye.‡

Already one can see the great divide between the besiegers and the besieged. The Prussians are disciplined, single-minded, and confident in their massive war-machine. The Parisians are volatile, feckless and unorganized, and indulging, still, in joie de vivre. They have learned little from Sedan. Strasbourg is besieged, and they are busy laying flowers at the feet of the statue of Strasbourg in the place de la Concorde.

Well had it been for Paris if she could have remained content with such artistic expression of patriotic feeling. Unfortunately the ridiculous usurped on the sublime. The statue of Strasbourg soon became grotesque with her shapeless *coiffure* of wreaths and garlands; the *gamin* performed his tumbles about her arms and hips; excited old gentlemen mounted on the pedestal, endeavouring to gain an audience; there was *Figaro*, too, with his tribute of praise, proposing to confer on the idol the cross of the Legion of Honour. Paris is in the feverish state of a man about to fight a duel: we puff at our cigar, flourish riding-whips, look at ourselves in the glass, and ask our seconds 'if they ever saw us so cool'.*

The comments were made by Henry Markheim, who later recorded his impressions under the pen-name of 'An Oxford Graduate'. They were substantiated by Henry Labouchère, the representative of the *Daily News* in Paris; he later published them as the *Diary of the Besieged Resident*. On 18 September, Labouchère observed that

no one walking on the Champs-Élysées or on the boulevards today would suppose that 300,000 Prussians are within a few miles of the city, and intend to besiege it ... Today is a fête day, and as a fête day it must be kept. Every one seems to have forgotten the existence of the Prussians. The cafés are crowded by a gay crowd. On the Boulevard, Monsieur and Madame walk quietly along with their children. In the Champs-Élysées honest mechanics and bourgeois are basking in the sun, and nurserymaids are flirting with soldiers. There is even a lull in the universal drilling ... Round the statue of Strasbourg there is the usual crowd ... I only saw one disturbance. As I passed by the

Rond Point, a very tall woman was mobbed, because it was thought that she might be a Uhlan in disguise. But it was regarded more as a joke than anything serious. So bent on being happy was every one that I really believe that a Uhlan in the midst of them would not have disturbed their equanimity.*

Mme Edgar Quinet, the wife of the historian and patriot, was equally out of touch with reality. She could not accept the fact that war was wholehearted.

The last telegraph lines of the Western region have been cut [she wrote in her journal on 18 September]. Paris is isolated. Here we are, separated from France and from the world . . .

Yesterday there was the first engagement in the Paris region, at Créteil. Who can sleep at the idea that the enemy is approaching? . . . The Parisians are setting fire to the woods round the city. The acrid smell of burnt forests lies heavy on your lungs. The sky is all red with the fire. How many sacrifices! France, they will count for you in the future. And Germany, who claims to represent civilization, is drunk with pride, and insults defenceless France . . .†

With the results of Forbach and Woerth to guide them, the generals entrusted with the defence of Paris could not leave the woods to stand [wrote Albert Vandam, in *An Englishman in Paris*]. But was there any necessity to destroy them in the way they did? In spite of the activity displayed, there were still thousands of idle hands anxious to be employed. Why were not the trees cut down and transported to Paris, for fuel for the coming winter? At that moment there were lots of horses available, and such a measure would have given us the double advantage of saving coals for the manufacture of gas, and of protecting from the rigours of the coming winter hundreds whose sufferings would have been mitigated by light and heat. Personally, I did not suffer much. From what I have seen during the siege, I have come to the conclusion that shortcomings in the way of food are far less hard to bear, nay, are almost cheerfully borne, in a warm room and with a lamp brightly burning. I leave out of the question the quantities in mineral oil wasted in the attempt to set fire to the woods, because of many instances the attempt failed utterly.*

A member of the Government, whom we met in the street a moment ago, told us [continued Mme Quinet] that the Prussians will easily capture the forts, but that Paris is impregnable in its walls of circum-vallation. They are making all haste to add a second ring of barricades inside; this commission for the barricades is presided over by Roche-fort and Flourens.†

It was odd, to say the least, that Henri de Rochefort-Luçay, better known as Henri Rochefort, the political journalist, should have been appointed to the post. It was not one which he seemed to relish.

Personally, as President of the Barricades Commission, I was the victim of a special kind of persecution. There was not a day when seven or eight Archimedes didn't come to suggest absolutely in-fallible ways of destroying the besieging army at a stroke. One of them had rediscovered Greek fire. No one has ever really known what this engine of destruction was made of, admitting that it ever did play a part in the mythological wars, but those for whom I refused to experi-ment on the Prussians with the new Greek fire very nearly called me a traitor . . .

Another man had a steam machine, which, launched at an irre-sistible speed through the enemy ranks, would cause untold ravages among them. It was no use exhausting myself by telling him that the enemy would get out of the way of the locomotive just as travellers get out of the way of those which they see approaching in the distance; it was no use, either, saying that it would be enough to climb a hill to make this so-called infernal machine completely inoffensive. I came up against arguments which had everything in their favour except reason, and this was enough to make them incontestable.‡

There were [continued Albert Vandam] inventors of impossible schemes for the instantaneous annihilation of the three hundred

thousand Germans around Paris, – inventors who supply the comic
note in the otherwise terrible drama, – inventors, who by day besiege
the Ministry of War, and to whom, after all, the minister's collabor-
ators are compelled to listen 'on the chance of there being something
in their schemes.'

'I am asking myself, every now and then, whether I am a staff-
officer or one of the doctors at Charenton,' said Prince Bibesca, one
evening.

'Since yesterday morning,' he went on, 'I have been interviewed
by a dozen inventors, every one of whom wanted to see General
Trochu or General Schmitz, and would scarcely be persuaded that
I would do as well. The first one simply took the breath out of me.
I had no energy left to resist the others, or to bow them out politely;
if they had chosen to keep on talking for four-and-twenty hours, I
should have been compelled to listen. He was a little man, about the
height of M. Thiers. His opening speech was in proportion to his
height; it consisted of one line. "Monsieur, I annihilate the Germans
with one blow," he said. I was thrown off my guard in spite of myself,
for etiquette demands that I should keep serious in spite of myself;
and I replied, "Let me fill my pipe before you do it."

'Meanwhile, my visitor spread out a large roll of paper on the table.
"I am not an inventor," he said; "I merely adapt the lessons of ancient
history to the present circumstances. I merely modify the trick of the
horse of Troy . . . "

'My second visitor had something not less formidable to propose;
namely, a sledgehammer, fifteen miles in circumference, and weighing
ten millions of tons. It was to be lifted up to a certain altitude by means
of balloons. A favourable wind had to be waited for, which would
send the balloons in the direction of Versailles, where the ropes
confining the hammer would be cut. In its fall it would crush and
bury the head-quarters and the bulk of the German army.

'The third showed me the plan of a musical mitrailleuse, which
would deal death and destruction while playing Wagner, Schubert,
and Mendelssohn, the former by preference. "The Germans", he

remarked, "are too fond of music to be able to resist the temptation of listening. They are sure to draw near in thousands when my mitrailleuses are set playing. We have got them at our mercy." I asked him to send me a small one as a sample; he promised to do so . . .'

By this time [wrote Vandam] we were shut off from the outer world. On 17 September, at night, the last train of the Orleans Railway Company had left Paris. The others had ceased working a day or so before, and placed their rolling stock in safety. Not the whole of it, though. A great many of the third-class carriages have had their seats taken out, the luggage and goods vans have been washed, the cattle trucks boarded in, and all these transformed into temporary dwellings for the suburban poor who have been obliged to seek shelter within the walls of the capital. The interiors of the principal railway stations present scenes that would rejoice the hearts of genre-painters on a large scale. The washing and cooking of all these squatters is done on the various platforms, the carriages have become parlour and bedroom in one, and there has even been some ingenuity displayed in their decoration. The womankind rarely stir from their improvised homes; the men are on the fortifications or roaming the streets of Paris. Part of the household goods has been stowed inside the trucks, the rest is piled up in front. The domestic pets, such as cats and dogs, have a particularly good time of it, for mice and rats abound, especially in the goods-sheds. Here and there a goat is gravely stalking along, happily unconscious of its impending doom; and chanticleer, surrounded by a small harem is trying to make the best of things.

Of course, the sudden and enormous influx of human beings could not be housed altogether in that way, but care has been taken that none of them shall be shelterless. All the tenantless apartments, from the most palatial in the Faubourg St Honoré and Champs-Élysées to the humblest in the popular quarters, have been utilized, and the pot-au-feu simmers in marble fireplaces, while Gallic Hodge sees his face reflected in gigantic mirrors the like of which he never saw before. The dwellings that have been merely vacated by their tenants who have flitted to Homburg and Baden-Baden, to Nice and elsewhere, are as yet not called into requisition.*

On 18 September the Institut de France drew up and published a declaration.

There is reason to fear that the armies which now surround the capital of France may be preparing to submit to all the hazards of a destructive bombardment the monuments which abound in it, the rarities of every kind, the masterpieces of every description . . .

We regret, once again, to impute such a thought to the German armies, the generals who lead them, the prince who is marching at their head.

If, nonetheless, and contrary to our expectation, this thought has been conceived; if this thought is to be realised: We, the members of the Institut de France, in the name of literature, the sciences, the arts, whose cause it is our duty to defend, denounce such a plan to the civilized world as an attack on civilization itself; we point it out to the justice of history; we offer it in advance to the avenging anger of posterity . . .†

The declaration, like much else about the Siege of Paris, was excellent theatre. It showed remarkable reluctance to accept the facts. France was at war. There was no reason why the enemy should not bombard the city they besieged, if they felt it tactically necessary. There was no reason to exempt Paris from the rules of warfare. But Parisians remained convinced that Paris was the centre of civilization. Albert de Lasalle could still enquire: 'Will people really believe, in the twentieth century, that bombs were filled in Berlin to set fire to the Conservatoire where Beethoven triumphs?'‡ Mme Quinet could still announce: 'The final battle is engaged beneath the walls of Paris. The cannon thunder, the circle of iron and fire embraces the holy city . . .'§

And so the Siege of Paris began. Perhaps the sharpest and most poignant comment on it was made by Jules Claretie in his book *La Guerre nationale*.

To any thinking man it is clear that the brutal separation, the fatal division which took place in France at the time of the Siege of Paris, were the cause of the catastrophes which followed. It is not healthy for a population of two million men to be enclosed for months on end. It is also dangerous for a nation to be separated for the same length of time from its capital. The trenches dug by the besieged army seem at once to make a single nation into two entirely different worlds.*

Part Two

Paris under
Siege

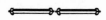

I *SEPTEMBER 1870*

The Siege of Paris, practically speaking, began on Monday, 19 September. As an anonymous chronicler wrote:

Paris was hemmed in by an impenetrable circle of iron, preventing all conveyance of intelligence. The railways had been cut, the Post-office was no longer able to transmit letters, and the telegraphic lines had ceased to act; in fact, the great French capital was as much debarred from communication with the outer world as if it had been all at once reduced to the very lowest degree in the scale of civilization.*

From 19 September, confirmed an un-named French observer,

it was impossible to leave the capital or to return to it, and the vast city remained isolated from the rest of France. And so began that siege, the most famous ever known to history, because of the greatness of the city and because of the extraordinary number of inhabitants which it contained. Within these walls, surrounded by the enemy armies, there were no less than 2,300,000 souls, who had to be fed with the resources accumulated in the city, and without receiving the slightest help from outside. The Prussians thought that Paris would not hold out for a fortnight.†

In fact the Prussians were not entirely sure of themselves. They considered the siege to be an audacious venture. Major William Blumé, of the Prussian Ministry of War, assessed the situation.

The force available for the investment of Paris on 19 September, consisted of six Army Corps, the Wurtemberg Division less one Brigade, and three Cavalry Divisions. As the troops had been incessantly advancing, it had not yet been possible to replace from the rear the very heavy casualties which had occurred; and the Corps had fallen so considerably below their proper establishment, that the army which carried out the investment of Paris on 19 September amounted only to some 122,000 Infantry, 24,000 Cavalry, and 622 guns.

The main enceinte of Paris has a circumference of about 4 miles, a line connecting the forts would be some 7½ miles long. The line of German outposts was 11 miles, and the line of telegraph, which connected the Headquarters of the several Corps, more than 20. Looking at these figures, and remembering the number of troops – badly organized though they were – which were in Paris at the time, it must be admitted that the investment was a bold undertaking. But the German leaders ventured on it without scruple, because they recognised that the surest way of forcing France to lay down her arms was to isolate and subdue the capital, *together with the considerable forces which had been collected in it*. There was one other way only besides this which could be taken into consideration – that of an attack, *de vive force*, to storm the place.

There was but little chance, however, of such an attack succeeding against a strong fortress consisting of outer forts and enceinte both storm-proof . . . To attempt an assault would, therefore, have been to risk the loss of all the great results already won; while, by adopting the plan of investment, a path was entered upon which would conduct surely, if slowly, to the desired end.*

An anonymous English author continued the chronicle:

Several small skirmishes had taken place between reconnoitring squads on both sides, but nothing of importance was reported till that afternoon [19 September]. About two o'clock, numbers of stragglers and deserters came up from the South. They were immediately surrounded by crowds of people anxious for news. The sum total of their statements was, that an engagement had taken place round Meudon, Clamart and Châtillon, and the French had been defeated. The enemy had, in the night, taken possession of the woods which the authorities had been unable to burn, owing to their dampness.

'Why were they not filled with French soldiers, then?' was the general question. These men as usual complained of bad generalship.

The news spread like wildfire, and the streets were soon crowded with mobs discussing the event.†

At three o'clock [wrote Henri Dabot, an advocate at the Cour d'appel], I saw the fire for the first time, from the top of the ramparts where I was on guard, at bastion no. 89, Porte d'Italie. The lights were coming from the direction of Montrouge and Châtillon. Alas! our soldiers were defeated; the runaways came down as far as the boulevard Saint-Michel, near the rue des Écoles. People thought that Paris had been captured, and that our battalion had been massacred on the ramparts.*

While Ducrot's men were fighting at Châtillon, Jules Favre, the Minister for Foreign Affairs, was discussing peace with Bismarck at Ferrières, fifteen miles to the east of Paris. He felt that peace on honourable terms had only to be asked for, provided that he could discover the right way of asking. He had unexpected support. Queen Victoria's marriage to Prince Albert of Saxe-Coburg-Gotha, and their eldest daughter's marriage to the Crown Prince of Prussia, made her largely German in sympathy. But she still remembered her triumphal state visit to Paris in 1855, and she still felt affection for the deposed Emperor and Empress. That day, 19 September, she sent her Foreign Secretary, Earl Granville, a private telegram in German for the King of Prussia.

The Queen asks the King of Prussia as a friend whether, in the interests of suffering humanity, he could so shape his demands as to enable the French to accept them. The King and his splendid victorious Army stand so high that the Queen thinks they can afford, on obtaining necessary securities for preventing similar events or attacks, to be generous. The King's name will stand even higher if he makes peace now.†

Favre, a skilful lawyer, was disillusioned by his venture. Far into the night he pleaded with Bismarck. Finally Bismarck gave him Prussia's demands: Alsace and part of Lorraine. Favre observed that no French Government could survive if it yielded to such terms. He accused Bismarck of wanting to destroy France. Then he wept.

Bismarck added that the Prussians would not even consider a temporary armistice unless the fortresses of Toul and Strasbourg – which were still holding out – were to surrender. The crushing interview was at an end.

On 25 September, from Berlin, the Queen of Prussia wrote to Queen Victoria:

Dearest Friend, . . . I approve very much your having telegraphed with dignity as well as tact to the King at the moment when first attempts at peace negotiations were about to be made . . .

The negotiations with Jules Favre have been in vain. The programme laid down in his circular, to which he probably adhered during the negotiation, i.e. starting with the condition of the integrity of French territory and of the fortresses, explains this result . . .

May God help us further! We must ever pray for an honourable and blessed peace.*

Meanwhile, round Paris, the Germans were waiting. On 20 September, from Versailles, Field-Marshal Count von Blumenthal recorded that 'the view from Mont de la Tour, looking completely over the city of Paris, is wonderfully fine, and we could hardly tear ourselves away from it. We derived special satisfaction from hearing some shells and shot which had been aimed at us fly harmlessly over our heads.'†

In Paris, Théophile Gautier took a ride on the inner circle railway. His account of his journey appeared in *Le Journal officiel*. It gave an artist's impression of a city which seemed poignantly beautiful at this oppressive moment in its history.

The Maison-Blanche station [wrote Gautier] is level with the route d'Italie. You go down to the railway, at the bottom of a cutting, by steps which are covered with a sheet-iron roof supported by cast-iron columns. We had taken seats on the top to enjoy a wider perspective, and the same idea had occurred to many other people, because there were very few travellers in the coaches. On the open seats on top there were militia, National Guards, bourgeois, sightseers, children and even women who had not been daunted by the ascent. Curiosity makes the daughters of Eve intrepid. Where would they not climb in the hope of seeing something? . . .

At many points in its course, the inner circle railway is quite deeply cut, and forms a trench within the city which might arrest the enemy, were he ever to penetrate so far. It is the outline of a third line of defence which must be completed, and people are working on it now. From our outside seat we saw the wheelbarrows passing above the railway cutting, the spades going up and down, men in shirtsleeves coming and going, and breastworks several yards thick being raised. General Totleben's precept of 'moving the earth' is being practised with a zeal which would delight the illustrious defender of Sebastopol.

Looking outwards, beyond the rampart, one saw, in a mist of luminous dust, the silhouette of the château de Bicêtre and the stern profile of the fort, which was firing at that moment. It was crowned with long billows of reddish smoke shot through by the sunlight. Casting one's eyes towards the city, one made out the meagre poplars which indicate the course of the Bièvre; one saw waste lands, enclosures fenced in with planks, stretches of leprous wall, tanners' sheds, washing hung out on lines, little gardens with a few autumn flowers, dahlias and sunflowers, pricking the landscape with points of red and yellow, market gardens spreading out their cabbage-patches, their salad beds, their lines of cloches sparkling like diamonds in the sun, the glass on their hotbeds sparking off sudden flashes of light.

Further on there glistened the pools of water of the Glacière, once patronised by skaters, at a time when the Bois de Boulogne had no lake. On the horizon, the Val-de-Grâce rounded out its dome, rather cramped and hump-backed like all buildings in the Louis XIII style, and the Panthéon, bolder and more elegant, raised its dome on a diadem of pillars. At the top of a hillock or rather of a rise in the ground there stood, in a picturesque way, the skeleton of a windmill with broken wings. This would have given Hoguet, the painter of windmills, freestone and felled trees, the subject for a pretty watercolour.

Gentilly is soon behind us . . . Passing the Montrouge and Vaugirard stations is the affair of a few minutes . . . The woods of lower
Meudon were turning yellow, gilded by the first cold winds, but
extremely gentle in tone and as if they were glimpsed through
silver gauze.

The whole horizon, moreover, was bathed in a white light in which
the contours were lost; and yet there was no fog, but rather a sort of
luminous dust. Nature that day seemed to be painted with the palette
of Corot.

The soul might have lost itself in dreams at this splendid sight.
As if to recall it to reality, some loud explosions which, this time,
did not come from the fort, were heard close at hand. The train
slowed down and began to cross the great Point-du-Jour viaduct,
which connects the two banks of the Seine.

From the top of this observatory, a marvellous panorama unfurled
before us. On one side, Paris with its domes, its towers, its distant
belfries, the river in the foreground, glazed with pearly reflections;
on the other, the gently undulating hills of Meudon, Bellevue and
Sèvres, velvety with bluish verdures; delightful promenades, fre-
quented by lovers in olden times . . . These hills are now hiding-
places for the Prussians, concealed in their shades like wild beasts.
There are our enemies, invisible by day and prowling at night at the
time when the predatory animals come out. No smoke betrays their
presence, nothing moves, no bayonet gleams. The solitude seems
complete, and you have to reason to persuade yourself that Paris is
besieged. Deceptive calm! In the shelter of these woods which the
autumn sap has saved from burning, the Prussians burrow in the
ground like moles; and, with blind tenacity, they remake the entrenchments which the shells from Mont-Valérien and the cannon-
balls from the gunboat Farcy destroy every morning.

The river was deserted. All one saw was an armoured gunboat towards the point of the île Saint-Germain; the lines of the stockades
of the defence traced three black bars across the water. To left and
right, below that, a long way down, for the top story of the viaduct,

across which the train is passing, is very high, there stretched the quays all bristling with obstacles which one need not describe.

While we were up there, the batteries of Auteuil and Point-du-Jour fired off some heavy shells; the uproar was doubled by the echoes of the arcades. It was the first time that we had heard the voice of the ramparts. It is a loud voice. It would make itself heard in a dialogue with the enemy.

If, contrary to their habits, we thought, the Prussians took it into their heads to answer, what a wonderful *objective* – may we for once use this fashionable *cliché*, which gives the war an appropriate and slightly aesthetic air – what a wonderful *objective* it would be for their shells, this train which had stopped, silhouetted clearly against the bright sky! And what a terrible fall our scattered remains would have from the top of this parapet to the bottom of the Seine! The same thought had no doubt occurred to several of our travelling companions. People had stopped laughing and chatting, and faces had assumed a grave expression. It was not without a certain satisfaction that one felt the train move on again.

Ronsard's elegy on the felled forest came back to our mind, at the sight of the poor Bois de Boulogne. The trees, cut wedgewise to within a few feet of the ground, form a herse of sharp stakes on which men and horses would be transfixed. A felled tree is a more melancholy sight than a demolished house. You need only money to rebuild a house. To make trees grow again, you need the slow collaboration of nature which, having eternity before her, is never hurried, and laughs at the impatience of ephemeral man; but Paris, which does not recoil from any sacrifice, has cut her fine green hair without regret, to be better suited to the fight, and not to give a hold to the foe.

Passing along the rampart, we look down into pleasant villas, charming retreats for a happy life. They have kept their marble fountains, their flowerbeds, their clumps of rare trees. At the edge of the avenue Uhrich we see the American field-ambulance installed in tents. This proved to be the best arrangement during the long War of Independence. Who would have thought, three months ago, that the flag of the International [Red Cross] Society would fly in the Bois de Boulogne, giving protection to the wounded?

The evening was beginning to fall, cold violet tints were filtering into the sky; things became blurred and their shapes grew indistinct. We had to postpone the rest of the excursion to another time. That day, unfortunately, the wind bore clouds heavy with rain, and a raging storm broke over the city, making the tiles and slates off the roofs fly like dead leaves. But we are an old traveller who has seen many storms, and we have a principle of never being concerned about the temperature, that eternal concern of the philistine. And so we set out in weather 'not to send a poet out of doors'.

We went back at first as far as Courcelles, where the Auteuil line connects with the inner circle railway. This part of the route is no less curious than the first. You go round the inside of the rampart, where there is the most picturesque activity. Casemates and armoured posts, shelters made of thick planks supported by stakes, rows of barrels filled with water and sand, hedges of faggots, sacks of earth set out on the parapet to protect the sentries: defences of every kind are multiplied to infinity. The walls of gardens and enclosures are crenelated, pierced with loopholes. Palisades bristle at the approaches to the stations; barricades made of paving stones, thick planks, tree trunks, present obstacles everywhere. Trenches lead from one to another . . .

Everything that the genius of desperate defence can imagine is accumulated there. We do not know if we shall go out of Paris, but certainly no one will come into it. There is nothing but embankments, trenches, escarps and counterscarps, sunk fences, caltrops, chevaux de frise, unpleasant surprises. There will have to be a battle to win every inch of earth. While they wait for the assault, the National Guards, the militia and the sharpshooters are keeping a keen lookout and listening intently; neither wind nor rain, nor mud, which puts yellow gaiters on their feet, affect their good humour in the least. They come and go, and exercise, light a fire for their cooking (with the North wind acting as bellows); they smoke their pipes, drink a glass of brandy at the canteen, and pay no heed to the rain, with which the aspersorium of the storm sprinkles their faces.*

On 20 September Mr Whitehurst, of the *Daily Telegraph*, also took the inner circle train. He visited Montrouge in search of copy.

We travelled third class on the roof [he informed his readers], to see what we could see. Indeed, we are now all 'sister Annes' every day, and truly we see clouds of dust. It was interesting as soon as we were clear of the city and could see the fortifications, inside which we travelled for some miles. There was a certain degree of activity in the works, but, as I think, not enough, and the authorities either cannot get workmen or they do not understand employing strong gangs and finishing off one operation at once.

There were plenty of materials – stone ready to hand for the strong works, heaps of sandbags, and stacks of fascines – but the men were wanting on the very day when every soldier not under fire should have been armed with a spade.†

Next day, 21 September, the author of *Life in Paris* continued:

The town by this time was very quiet, but tolerably gay. What a change in two short months! People who lived in Paris could scarcely realise it, for the change had come upon them gradually. The public gardens, instead of being merry with the voices of children, were full of artillery. Arms were piled in every street. Everybody was a soldier. Even the waiters and cab-drivers were in uniform. All the churches and theatres were turned into ambulances and barracks. The new Opera House had been inaugurated . . . One wing was a hospital, another a police-station, a third a barrack, while the upper part was full of stores of all kinds . . . Most of the Paris priests had joined the ambulance corps. All did likewise, who wished to avoid annoyance and suspicion, for it was dangerous to be in civilian dress. Everybody was expected to do something for the defence of the capital.‡

Parisians were increasingly tense. That same day Henry Labouchère found everyone engaged in measuring the distance from the Prussian batteries to his particular house.

One friend I found seated in a cellar with a quantity of mattresses over it, to make it bomb-proof. He emerged from his subterraneous Patmos, to talk to me, ordered his servant to pile on a few more mattresses, and then retreated. Anything so dull as existence here it is difficult to imagine. Before the day is out one gets sick and tired of the one single topic of conversation. We are like the people at Cremorne waiting for the fireworks to begin; and I really do believe that if this continues much longer, the most cowardly will welcome the bombs as a relief from the oppressive ennui.*

There was suspicion as well as nervousness and oppressive boredom. That day an eloquent statement appeared in the Press.

A number of coachmen, who were driving their carriages, have been threatened and even attacked, on the pretext that they should be carrying rifles rather than whips; that they could only be bad citizens.

The service which they perform cannot be interrupted; indeed, it is indispensable, not only from the point of view of circulation in Paris, but because of the transport of the wounded and other missions to be accomplished in the interest of defence and for the needs of the Republic.

They are therefore set under the protection of the authorities, who will if need be support them against anyone who tries to disturb or hinder a service of public interest.†

It was not only coachmen who suffered from the general suspicion. That evening Victor Hugo reported that a crowd, 'mingled with soldiers and *gardes mobiles*, was looking up at the corner of the rue des Martyrs, at the fifth floor of a tall house, at the comings and goings of lights which seemed to be signals. There were cries of anger. They were about to search the house . . .'‡

Henry Markheim, the Oxford Graduate, recorded later in the autumn that the spy-fever has somewhat cooled down; but it is still unsafe, particularly if you chance to live on a fourth or fifth story, to read a novel in bed by the light of a lamp with a green-coloured shade; for the chances are that, before you have got as far as the description of the heroine, a band of National Guardsmen will burst into the room, drag you out of bed, and accuse you of being a spy and corresponding with the Prussians by means of coloured signals. I had myself a narrow escape the other day when I strolled up the hill of Montmartre to enjoy the view of the surrounding country. A taste for scenery creates suspicion in the patriotic breast, especially at Montmartre; and before I had been many minutes watching the sunshine on the hills, a citizen came up and said he should like to know where *monsieur* lived, because it seemed to him that *monsieur* did not belong to the *quartier*; and then he wondered what could bring *monsieur* up such a steep hill merely to look at the country. Immediately I found myself surrounded by a posse of National Guards, one of whom unfortunately remembered that he had seen me pass *twice* in the same street in front of the *Mairie*, and that was strange, very strange indeed. I was lost unless I made a speech; so I plucked up courage and began. 'Citizens, I shall only be too happy to answer all your questions; but first let me tell you how much I admire your watchfulness: our friends at the Federal Chamber will be proud to hear that Montmartre keeps such a vigilant eye on traitors. Our worst enemy is the Reaction.' Before I could proceed any further with my harangue the 'citizens' interrupted me with profuse apologies, which I had the generosity to accept, and hastened to remove myself to some less *national-guarded* spot.*

The Oxford Graduate was still prepared to stay in Paris and to write *Inside Paris during the Siege*. Henry Labouchère was content to stay in Paris as the Besieged Resident. Some of their compatriots were, however, anxious to go home. On 22 September Labouchère recorded:

Just now I saw drawn up in the courtyard of the Grand Hotel a travelling carriage, with hampers of provisions, luggage, and an English flag flying. Into it stepped four Britons. Their passports were viséd, they said, by their Embassy, and they were starting for England via Rouen. Neither French nor Prussians would, they were convinced, stop them. I did not even confide a letter to their hands, as they are certain, even if they get through the French outposts, to be arrested by the Prussians and turned back.*

Labouchère's predictions were well founded. Next day, at Ferrières, Dr Moritz Busch, one of Bismarck's staff, reported:

After breakfast I receive a number of English letters from Paris, which have been seized, the contents of which I am to make use of mostly to the newspapers. There is, however, very little of interest for our press. Lamentations on the damage done to the beautiful boulevards, on the attacks of the people upon the generals of the Empire . . .†

There were now, it seemed, only two ways for Paris to communicate with the outside world: by carrier pigeon and by balloon. Photographic reductions of messages were attached to the pigeons' tails, and the birds were hopefully released to fly out of the range of the Prussian gunfire.

The first photographic reductions on paper measured 2 inches by $1\frac{1}{2}$, and contained 240 ordinary despatches; the collodion films carried much more, each small page of print, containing 15,000 characters or about 200 despatches, being reduced to a mere speck, in fact a parallelogram measuring superficially about *one twenty-fifth of a square inch* . . . Finally, 15,000 ordinary messages and 500 pages of official despatches were contained in a small quill attached to the tail feather of the pigeon; some carrying as many as twenty-three films of collodion. Numerous copies, sometimes as many as fifty, were sent by different birds. In all, nearly 100,000 despatches were sent to Paris, but the proportion received was very small; many of the birds had a long way to fly, and a great number were doubtless shot or killed by birds of prey.‡

The postal authorities also entrusted letters to balloonists; and during the siege they sent out fifty-four balloons, which took about 2,500,000 letters with them. The first of these balloons took off on 23 September. A French staff-officer described the occasion.

Today saw the inauguration of the first successful attempt to apply ballooning to the transport of despatches, by the departure of a *post-balloon*, chartered by the administration of postal services. It was the *Neptune*, taken up by M. Durouf, collaborator of M. Nadar, which inaugurated the series of these aerial messengers, entrusted with taking our provincial brethren and the relations we have sent far away, the echoes of our affection and our patriotic hopes.

At 7 o'clock precisely, a carriage from the administration of postal services set down several enormous sealed mailbags. M. Rampont, director of posts, the directorate of telegraphs, several members of the defence commission and some senior officers were present.

The *Neptune*, a balloon which cubes twelve hundred metres, had been permanently inflated day and night, for seventeen days, for an endless series of observation ascents. Despite this long, hard service, the ropes of the net were so taut that they made the rim of the basket crack, and the *Neptune* was in a hurry to go.

The manoeuvre was performed by the former crew of *Le Géant*, who have long been attached to the fortunes of Nadar. The members of this crew had an excellent appearance, and bore no relation to the usual followers of performing aeronauts; they were assisted by eight sailors and twenty-five soldiers of the line.

At quarter-past seven, the loading was finished. For this first departure Nadar had chosen M. Durouf, already celebrated for his maritime ascents at Cap Gris-Nez and Monaco. M. Durouf gave the sacramental order: 'Let's go!' and the balloon had hardly left the ground before the aeronaut's cry: 'Vive la République!' was answered by the early morning crowd, assembled in the place Saint-Pierre, with unanimous applause.

The *Neptune* had soon reached a height of 1500 metres, the region which had been indicated for its route, and it went straight in the direction of Calvados. The wind gave it a speed of 15 leagues an hour. It carried, besides the aeronaut, a load of two hundred kilos of despatches on thin paper, and a considerable ballast.*

The venture amazed Thomas Gibson Bowles, the special correspondent of the *Morning Post* in Paris.

If anybody had told me three months ago that on this day [24 September] I should be walking along the boulevards seriously considering of sending letters to England by balloon, I should have avoided the prophet as a dangerous lunatic; yet that is precisely what I have just been doing. Since Sunday last we have been entirely isolated, and although this is perhaps of all places in the world that in which isolation is least felt, yet to those who have been accustomed to read their newspapers and get their tradesmen's bills with a touching regularity, it is a novel sensation, and not altogether pleasing, to feel that one is out of reach for an altogether indefinite time equally of *Times* and tailors . . .

The one irritating feature about being thus shut up is that, so far, we have not had any excitement to justify it all. Not a bomb has fallen, not a horse has been eaten as yet, and one's dinner costs just the same money and consists of precisely the same elements that it always did.†

Thomas Bowles was more fortunate in his eating than Edmond de Goncourt:

In the capital of fresh food and first fruits [wrote the diarist], it is really ironic to catch the Parisians consulting one another outside the tin-plate counters of cosmopolitan merchants and grocers. Finally they decide to go in, and they come out with *Boiled Mutton*, *Boiled Beef*, etc., under their arms, every possible and impossible preserved meat and vegetable, things that one would never have thought would become the food of rich Parisians . . .

The restaurant menus are shrinking. They ate the last oysters yesterday; and, as far as fish is concerned, there is nothing left but eel and gudgeon.*

24 September, 4 o'clock pm

We have been in a state of wild enthusiasm all this afternoon [recorded Labouchère]. At about 1 o'clock it was rumoured that 20,000 Prussians and 40 cannon had been taken. There had been a heavy firing, it was said, this morning, and a Prussian force had approached near the forts of Ivry and Bicêtre. General Vinoy had issued forth from Vincennes, and, getting behind them, had forced them under the guns of the forts, where they were taken prisoners. The Boulevards immediately were crowded; here a person announcing that he had a despatch from the front, here another vowing he had been there himself. Wherever a drum was heard there was a cry of 'Here come the prisoners!' Tired of this, at about 4 o'clock I drove to Montrouge. It is a sort of Parisian Southwark. I found all the inhabitants lining the streets, waiting, too, for news. A regiment marched in, and there was a cry that it had come from the front; then artillery filed out of the city gate. I tried myself to pass, and had got half-way through before I was stopped, then I was turned back. The prisoners here, close by the scene of action, had dwindled down to 5,000. Imagine Southwark, with every man armed in it, and a battle going on at Greenwich, and you will have an idea of the excitement of Montrouge . . .

25 September

No news of any importance from the front. It is a fête day, but there are few holiday makers. The presence of the Prussians at the gates, and the sound of the cannon, have at last sobered this frivolous people. Frenchmen, indeed, cannot live without exaggeration, and for the last twenty-four hours they have taken to walking about as if they were guests at their own funerals. It is hardly in their line to play the *justum et tenacem* of Horace. Always acting, they are now acting the part of Spartans. It is somewhat amusing to see the stern gloom on the face of patriots one meets, who were singing and shouting a few days ago – more particularly as it is by no means difficult to distinguish beneath this outward gloom a certain keen relish, founded upon the feeling that the part is well played. One thing, however, is certain, order has at length been evolved from disorder. Except in the morning, hardly any armed men are to be seen in the streets, and even in the central Boulevards, except when there is a report of some success or during an hour in the evening, there are no crowds. In the fighting faubourgs there is a real genuine determination to fight it out to the last. The men there have arms, and they have not cared to put on uniforms. Men, women, and children are all of one mind in the quarters of the working men. I have been much struck with the difference between one of these poor fellows who is prepared to die for the honour of his country, between his quiet, calm demeanour, and the absurd airs, and noisy brawls, and the dapper uniforms of the young fellows one meets with in the fashionable quarters. It is the difference between reality and sham, bravery and bombast . . .

Evening (Sunday)
They could stand it no longer; the afternoon was too fine. Stern patriotism unbent, and tragic severity of demeanour was forgotten. The Champs-Élysées and the Avenue de la Grande Armée were full of people. Monsieur shone by his absence; he was at the ramparts, or was supposed to be there; but his wife, his children, his *bonne*, and his kitchen wench issued forth, oblivious alike of dull care and of bombarding Prussians, to enjoy themselves after their wont by gossiping and lolling in the sun. The Strasburg fetish had its usual crowd of admirers. Every bench in the Champs-Élysées was occupied. Guitars twanged, organs were ground, merry-go-rounds were in full swing, and had it not been that here and there some regiment was drilling, one would have supposed oneself in some country fair. There were but few men; no fine toilets, no private carriages. It was a sort of Greenwich-park. At the Arc de Triomphe was a crowd trying to discover what was going on upon the heights above Argenteuil. Some declared they saw Prussians, while others with opera glasses declared

that the supposed Prussians were only trees. In the Avenue de l'Impératrice was a large crowd gazing upon the Fort of Mont Valérien. This fort, because I presume it is the strongest for defence, is the favourite of the Parisians. They love it as a sailor loves his ship. 'If I were near enough,' said a girl near me, 'I would kiss it.' 'Let me carry your kiss to it,' replied a Mobile, and the pair embraced, amid the cheers of the people round them. At Auteuil there were *fiacres* full of sightseers, come to watch the Prussian batteries at Meudon, which could be distinctly seen. Occasionally, too, there came a puff of smoke from one of the gunboats.*

That same day, 25 September, the Oxford Graduate recorded:

We have had three days' 'manifesting', one day's victory, seven days' siege; perhaps we deserve our *dimanche*. The weather is so wonderfully fine it makes one forget the Prussians, who will, no doubt, retaliate by forgetting us – such is their respect for the Sabbath. Besides, the siege has already lasted a week, and that is a long time for anything to occupy the thoughts of a Parisian. We cannot always be talking of bombardments, of blowing ourselves up, and making Paris the grave of her enemies . . . ; the best thing, meanwhile, is to make of it as pleasant a place as the Parisians and Belleville will admit.†

Parisians tried in vain to make their city a pleasant place. Felix Whitehurst continued:

Such a bear-garden as the Champs-Élysées today [25 September] I have never seen! The people sat just where they have been told not to sit for years. They have destroyed every flower, trodden the turf to dust, and scattered old newspapers and empty bottles all over the ornamental parts of the show-thoroughfare of Paris. It was like a bad fair. Goat-carriages and go-carts, merry-go-rounds, Mobiles playing billiards for almond-cakes, nursery maids neglecting their charges for the tender passion (of course 'Mars' in the ascendant), an arrest here, a fight there, a chorus of 'Mourir pour la Patrie' from

half-drunken lips, and when there was a lull the cannon of Mont
Valérien murmured hoarsely in the distance. This cannot be Paris!

. . . [The Prussians] have 300,000 men within twenty-five miles of
Paris . . .*

On 26 September Thomas Bowles confirmed:

There must be a large number of people in the world who take no
account at all of what is going on in it. Thus I see the usual number
of elderly individuals, in equally elderly coats and linen, occupying
themselves daily with the exciting sport of fishing for gudgeon from
the quays. They have fished for years under all kinds of *régimes*, without troubling themselves about changes of Government, and probably will continue to fish till the bombs begin to fall about them . . . I
am sure there is scarcely a Parisian who really thinks it possible, even
now, that a bomb can fall on the sacred boulevards. Projectiles are
getting nearer, however, in their course. This evening the Prussians
fired a few long shots from the heights of Châtillon, and sent some of
them very nearly inside the fortifications – very nearly, but not quite.
It is expected that the attack will soon commence.†

That day, at Bismarck's headquarters, Dr Moritz Busch reported:

It is asserted that Paris, with its collections, fine buildings and monuments, must not be bombarded: that it would be a crime against
civilization. Why not indeed? Paris is a fortress. That there are within
it treasures of art, splendid palaces, and other fine things, does not
alter its character. A fortress is an apparatus of war, which must be
rendered harmless, without reference to what is involved in doing
so.‡

Théophile Gautier to his daughter:

29 September

My dear Estelle,

As the highways are cut off one must have recourse to the airways,
and I am entrusting my letter to the first balloon to take off. We are

shut in, separated from the rest of the world, and it is very cruel not to have any news of the people you love. I am well; Lili and Zoé [your aunts] are getting used to the situation and they aren't too bad. Nothing serious has happened yet, and one is in a perpetual and feverish state of expectation . . . I spend most of my time at the *Officiel* reading newspapers which are usually printed on half-sheets for want of paper or want of copy. I am very vexed not to see you, dear child, and yet I don't wish that you were with me, because this way of life lacks all gaiety. What a pity it is to be a prisoner like this, while the weather is so wonderful! The sky seems to defy us by decking itself in its most ironically brilliant blue velvet. How beautiful the Lake [of Geneva] must be! Take advantage of your leisure and paint a big and really careful watercolour. I only wish I could go and wish a happy St Charles to Carlotta, as I usually do, and bring you back to Paris after a brief stay, but really I hardly dare to hope for this. The future is absolutely undecipherable. In the meanwhile, do give an affectionate kiss to your dear aunt and your nice cousin for me, and, as for you, accept two big fatherly kisses in the old-fashioned style.

The author of your days

THÉOPHILE GAUTIER*

Night of 29–30 September

After my sentry-duty [wrote Henri Dabot], I lay down to have a rest, with my right ear on the ground. Suddenly I clearly made out the sound of gun-carriages. They seemed to be going out through the neighbouring gates at Choisy and Bicêtre; were we going to attack the Prussians?

At ten past five in the morning, a cannon shot made us all run on to the talus of the fortifications. The fort at Ivry was cannonading the Prussian lines, while the fort at Montrouge was shelling them. Ahead of us, the Prussians encamped at L'Hay, at Chevilly and in the cemetery at Choisy (alas, near the tomb of Rouget de l'Isle!) answered energetically.

We could see the flash of their cannon wonderfully well and we were deafened by the fearful noise which followed the flash a few seconds later. Soon there was a sinister, crackling sound like a coffee-grinder; the machine-guns were claiming their own. I went towards the Porte d'Italie, and saw a multitude of ambulance waggons and mule-litters going out.

Half an hour later the mule-litters came back laden with wounded. What a lamentable sight!*

30 September

We are still beating our tom-toms like the Chinese, to frighten away the enemy, and our braves still fire off powder at invisible Uhlans. The Prussians, to our intense disgust, will not condescend even to notice us. We jeer at them [wrote Labouchère], we revile them, and yet they will not attack us. What they are doing we cannot understand. They appear to have withdrawn from the advanced positions which they held. We know that they are in the habit of making war in a thoroughly ungentlemanly manner, and we cannot make up our minds whether our 'attitude' is causing them to hesitate, or whether they are devising some new trick to take us by surprise. That they are starving, that their communications with Germany are cut off, that their leaders are at loggerheads, that the Army of the Loire will soon be here to help us to demolish them, we have not the slightest doubt. The question is no longer whether Paris will be taken – that we have solved already; it is whether the Prussians will be able to get back to the Rhine. We are thankful that Bismarck did not accept Jules Favre's offer of a money indemnity. We would not give a hundred francs now to ensure peace or an armistice. I went this morning into a shop, the proprietor of which, a bootmaker, I have long known, and I listened with interest to the conversation of this worthy man with some of his neighbours who had dropped in to have a gossip, and to congratulate him on his martial achievements, as he had been on guard in a bastion. We first discussed why the Army of the Loire had not arrived, and we came to the conclusion that it was engaged in rallying Bazaine. 'I should like to read your English newspapers now,' said one; 'your *Tims* [sic] told us we ought to cede Alsace and Lorraine, but its editor must now acknowledge that Paris is invincible.' I told him that I felt convinced that he did so regularly every morning. 'No peace,' shouted a little tailor, who had been prancing about on an imaginary steed, killing imaginary Prussians, 'we have made a pact with death; the world knows now what are the consequences of attacking us.' The all-absorbing question of subsistence then came up, and some one remarked that beef would give out sooner than mutton. 'We must learn', observed a jolly-looking grocer, 'to vanquish the prejudices of our stomach. Even those who do not like mutton must make the sacrifice of their taste to their country.' I mildly suggested that perhaps in a few weeks the stomachs which had a prejudice against rats would have to overcome it. At this the countenance of the gossips fell considerably, when the bootmaker, after mysteriously closing the door, whispered: 'A secret was confided to me this morning by an intimate friend of General Trochu. There is a tunnel which connects Paris with the provinces, and through it flocks and herds are entering the town.' This news cheered us up amazingly.*

At the beginning of October, the Prussians held the palace of Saint-Cloud, and they were busy constructing batteries and digging trenches on the platform of La Lanterne de Diogène: a high point in the park, which commanded Paris.

It was evident that they would not make an attack on Paris till they had got up their monster siege guns, and if they could get them up to the Lanterne, the position of the south-west of Paris was critical. From the Lanterne to the towers of Notre-Dame (the spot . . . from which all distances from Paris are calculated), it is exactly five miles as the crow flies. From this the reader can infer what would have been the consequence of a battery of Krupp's monster ordnance planted on that platform.*

On 1 October, Dr Moritz Busch reported that at dinner 'we had Count Waldersee [the German general] as our guest. He wishes Paris, as a Sodom which corrupts the world, to be thoroughly humbled.'†

Humbled it already was.

As regards the state of Paris [wrote an anonymous observer], the apparent inaction of the enemy was making people feel very nervous . . . The absence of any news from abroad was felt to be more irksome than the cutting off of even those luxuries which to Parisians are dearer than the necessaries of life.

The favourite meal of Parisians of every age, sex, and degree, café au lait, had become impossible, there being no milk to be had for love or money. Eggs fetched the absurd price of 10d (1f each), and butter was in demand at 3f a pound.‡

On 1 October, Edmond de Goncourt recorded:

Yesterday, at Peters, they brought me some roast beef. I examined the watery meat, without fat, striped with white sinews; my artist's eyes looked at the blackish red, so different from the pink red of beef. The waiter only insisted very half-heartedly that this horse was beef.§

It was not only food that had changed; the whole appearance and way of life of Paris was already different.

The gilded cupola of the Invalides [added the author of *Life in Paris*] was about this time covered by a tarpaulin, under the impression that the gilding would make it a target, and the windows of the Louvre were protected by sandbags . . .

On the Boulevards most cafés shut at nine o'clock, and by ten the streets and Boulevards were empty and silent . . . All that made life pleasant in Paris had ceased to exist. Business was at a standstill. The streets had not been watered, there was a heavy pall of dust hovering above the city – and drilling, the rattle of the drum, and the booming of distant cannon were the only sounds that disturbed the silence.*

A deathly silence [recorded Théophile Gautier], a terrifying solitude along the quai. You would think you were in a medieval city, at the hour when curfew sounds. You can just hear the rumble of a carriage in the distance, or the steps of a bourgeois going home. The houses rise up tall and dark, silhouetting their roofs against the night like black velvet on black cloth. Only three windows are lit up from the corner of the quai Voltaire to the cupola of the Institut. Near the rank inspector's kiosk there trembles the lantern of a last cab. The street lamps, dimly lit, prick the darkness with occasional red points. Their reflections lengthen and dissolve in the river like tears of blood. But suddenly the capricious wind blows aside the clouds, and lights up as many stars in heaven as it extinguishes gas-jets on earth. All the illumination is on above!†

On 1 October Thomas Gibson Bowles, of the *Morning Post*, had an interview with Jules Favre,

who bears the stamp of a remarkable man upon him . . . I may say, without indiscretion [wrote Bowles], that the Government attaches great importance to the attitude of England, and hopes for her sympathy and moral support in the trials through which the country is

passing; though it would appear to share the disappointment expressed throughout French society at the coldness, not to say grati-
fication, with which the English Cabinet and a part of the English
Press have looked on while France has been engaged in a struggle for
mere existence.*

French disappointment was clearly reflected in that day's issue of *Le
Journal Officiel*. It published a long proclamation by Louis Blanc, the
left-wing politician and historian. This was addressed 'To the English
People'; it was a curious mixture of despair and arrogance.

Civilization [Blanc explained] is, at the moment, a prisoner in Paris.
That was the ultimate exploit dreamed of by the King of Prussia.
The nineteenth century has its Attila. He and his advisers, with blood
up to their knees, invoking what they call the God of armies, have
sworn that the great, beloved city, the permanent meeting-place of all
the peoples of the world, should be for the moment cut off from the
world; that the city of all Europe should suddenly be lacking from
Europe; that, in one of the principal laboratories of thought, thought
should be stifled between the cannon; that Paris, the capital of cos-
mopolitanism, should, for a while, be like an island – an island no
longer having even the Ocean to help it to live the life of the world.
So be it, then . . .

All that I want to prove to the English people is this: our cause is
just . . .

If the English people understand that our cause is that of the whole
world, since it is that of justice, it is for them to act in consequence;
it is for them to consider, as far as it concerns them, the results of
the unbounded right of conquest. A nation that sanctions, by its in-
difference, the saturnalia of force, risks suffering them itself, and it
deserves them.†

But England was determined, now, not to intervene. That day,
Queen Victoria wrote explicitly to her Foreign Secretary:

Balmoral, 1 October 1870. The Queen is so glad to see how firmly and *resolutely* Lord Granville refused to be dragged *into* mediation and interference, though it must be very difficult to avoid it.

The Queen feels so very *strongly* the danger *to this country* of giving advice which will not help the *one* party, and may turn the very powerful other party, already much (and unjustly) irritated against us, into an inveterate enemy of England, which would be very dangerous and serious.

She also feels that, if we offer advice, we shall be asked to give promises for eventual action one way or another, which may be very serious for us and drag us into intervention; for we could not say, if we pressed our advice, that we would on no account act.*

One Frenchman was determined to act. Next day Victor Hugo issued another proclamation, couched in his most oracular style. It was addressed, this time, to the people of Paris.

. . . Resistance today; deliverance tomorrow; that is all. We are no longer flesh, we are stone. I no longer know my name, I am called France, Paris, wall!

How beautiful our city will be! Let Europe expect to see the impossible; let her expect to see Paris grow greater . . .

The Panthéon wonders how it can receive this whole population which will be entitled to its dome . . . And, henceforward, every time that Prussia attacks, while the mitrailleuse is roaring, what shall we see in the streets? We shall see women smiling. O Paris, you have crowned the statue of Strasbourg with flowers; history will crown you with stars.†

Some of the sharpest, most immediate observations on Paris under siege came from Edwin Child: a young Londoner of twenty-four who was working in a clock shop at 5, rue Scribe. On 2 October he confided in his diary:

. . . Whoever had said 3 months ago that a Provincial paper a fortnight old, arriving in Paris, would cause a sensation, would have been laughed at, however, such was the case Thursday, the *Journal de Rouen* being published *in extenso* in the current number of the *Gaulois*, such gives a convincing proof of the progress of civilization in the 19th century, already, it is 21 days that 2,000,000 people in the richest, loveliest, gayest, most cosmopolitan, most hospitable and most insouciant town in the world, have been without any news from the outer world, may the lesson not be lost upon others.*

News from the outer world came all too soon, and it was devastating news. Toul had been captured; and on 27 September, after a gallant defence, and after savage bombardment by the Prussians, Strasbourg had finally surrendered. On 3 October a French staff-officer recorded:

The weather is magnificent, and the sunshine is as brilliant as can be! One revolts inside oneself against nature which is so radiant and beautiful when around us, and in our souls, all should be mourning and grief. Many flowers are scattered at the feet of the statue of Strasbourg in the place de la Concorde; and many tears are repressed!†

Toul and Strasbourg have surrendered, no doubt for lack of food and munitions [added a more practical naval officer]. Let us pay tribute to their constancy, but let us postpone till happier times all these idle manifestations in their honour. Let us think about making our defence more effective than theirs; we have only to stamp on the ground, and men and arms will rise up from it. Paris is overflowing with an activity which may later become a subject of real anxiety if it is not controlled. We must use it; we must attack the enemy with mines and entrenchments. Two hundred thousand workers may, in their turn, besiege the enemy in its own lines. Until now, alas! we are agitating, we are not advancing.

We lack rifles; we lack artillery; we lack projectiles. In order to save munitions, the forts are silent, and the enemy can circulate freely within reach of their guns. We don't lack workmen and engineers. But the artillery is loath, they say, to hand over a model of machine-guns or campaign-guns, to private industry. To satisfy public opinion, they have had to content themselves with ordinary Christophe and Gattling machine-guns which are mediocre while they wait for the war to allow them to see the Meudon model, which is excellent. Why not break such resistance? Why these wretched discussions of price-lists which have arisen, so they say, between the administration and the makers? Doesn't time have its value as well?*

Captain Hozier, an English observer, added that 'the supply of work-men was very inadequate. Once taken away from the foundry or workshop, numbers of men preferred idleness and fifteen pence [Government allowance] a day to hard work with three times that amount of pay; it was with great difficulty that hands enough were found for the casting of cannon, the transformation of muskets, the repair of arms, and the manufacture of ammunition of various kinds.'†

On 4 October Felix Whitehurst 'went to see Countess Rapp's private hospital for the wounded. I saw eight patients', he recorded, 'who must really thank the God of Battles for getting them shot. The house, in the rue Cardinal Fesch, is wonderfully airy, cool, and comfortable. The Countess sits up three nights a week with her patients, and they are attended by international surgeons. France ought really to be very proud of these semi-French, who do so much for them.'‡ The American lady, Mrs Griffin, was not to be outdone:

On the Avenue de l'Impératrice we found the snowy tents of *our* ambulance scattered over a large extent of ground. It looked very picturesque amid the trees and grass, and the 'Stars and Stripes' floating over it from the centre or principal tent. We entered, and the first person we met was Mr Washburne (junior), son of the American Minister, who politely received us, showed us over the ambulance, and explained to us the various departments and their uses. The beds of the invalids were very clean, while the convalescents seemed kindly cared for. Some were reading, while others were listening. All was order and perfect neatness. There were many lady visitors, amongst the number Madame Trochu and her daughter, who manifested great interest.*

Henri Dabot, the Parisian advocate, noted acidly: 'Visited the American ambulance. A lady of the most gracious kind was acting as sister of charity ... in pearl grey gloves.'†

There are in Paris [wrote Labouchère] two hundred and forty-three ambulances, and when the siege commenced, such was the anxiety to obtain a *blessé*, that when a sortie took place, those who brought them in were offered bribes to take them to the house over which the flag of Geneva waved. A man with a broken leg or arm was worth thirty francs to his kind preservers. The largest ambulance is the International. Its headquarters are at the Grand Hotel. It seems to me over-manned, for the number of the healthy who receive pay and rations from its funds exceeds the number of the wounded. Many, too, of the former are young unmarried men, who ought to be serving either in the ranks of the army, or at least of the Garde Nationale. The following story I take from an organ of public opinion: A lady went to her Mairie to ask to be given a wounded soldier to look after. She was offered a swarthy Zouave. 'No,' she said, 'I wish for a blonde, being a brunette myself.'‡

It was all somewhat unreal. As O'Shea observed:

There were too many toy ambulances in Paris, and too few serious ones, attended by persons who were earnest enough to try to know their business, industrious enough to do it, and modest enough to take duty as its own reward ...

'Doctor, do send us a wounded man, like a dear!' was not an unusual petition.

The doctor could not always oblige, and the gentle creatures had often to put up with a private of the Mobiles suffering from swollen feet, when they had been hoping for a cavalry colonel, pale and interesting, seamed with a scar from a Uhlan's lance.§

Among the gentle creatures who hoped for a cavalry colonel we may safely list Sarah Bernhardt, who was 'very busy with the hospital at the Théâtre de l'Odéon'.*

On 5 October, Édouard Thierry, the General Administrator of the Comédie-Française, recorded in his diary:

There still isn't any meat today . . .

Saw Théophile Gautier pass, and ran to catch up with him outside the theatre, where we talked to M. Chabrol. Théophile Gautier will come and pay us a visit, since there is still a meeting-place at the Théâtre-Français.

Asked M. Chabrol if he would have a cellar where we could put the statue of Voltaire. He thought that the statue was safe enough in one of our corridors. He saw no danger where it was, unless there was a volley of musketry which shattered our windows. As for the bombardment, he doesn't believe that it will happen; anyway, the Prussian shells couldn't reach us.†

Théophile Gautier kept his promise to visit the theatre. He described the occasion in *Tableaux de Siège*.

The flag of the International [Red Cross] Society, with its cross of gules on an argent field, flies from the roof of the theatre and from the balcony where you go to snatch a breath of fresh air during the intervals. Wounded men are lying in the foyer which was once paced by the critics, sometimes so lost in discussion that they forgot the play. At first sight, there is nothing so strange as this proximity of hospital and stage, but we live in a time of sudden contrasts. The most unexpected antitheses are created by events . . .

From the great stage-box which was once the Imperial box, the casualties from the field-hospital, now convalescent, were watching the performance. All eyes were turned towards them with compassion. There were arms in slings, there were hands and heads swathed in bandages; but the person who drew most attention was a young man with a broad bandage across his face. He looked like one of those

Touaregs of the Sahara who veil their faces up to the eyes like women. A bullet had lodged in the wing of his nose, and it was said that the doctors had not been able to take it out yet. This did not prevent him from paying close attention to Andromaque's tears and Hermione's rages . . .

We gladly accepted Édouard Thierry's suggestion that we took a stroll round the foyer, that is to say the field-hospital. It is in fact in this splendid airy room, with its lofty ceiling and easy access, combining all the conditions of salubrity, that the field-hospital is installed. The monumental fireplace, in front of which there have been so many discussions, warms the room with its enormous logs and keeps it at a gentle temperature. The beds of the wounded are set out with their heads to the wall on each side of the foyer, leaving a wide passage between them. The busts of the tragic and comic poets look at them with their stony eyes and seem to watch over them. Houdon's Voltaire is still chuckling in his marble armchair. No veil has been cast over the patriarch of Ferney; only a strip of green chintz protects his pedestal . . .

There is no need to say that these beds are meticulously clean and dazzlingly white. Other beds have been set out in the long gallery which used to serve as a promenade: the gallery whose windows open on to the balcony in the rue Richelieu. On the last of these beds, no doubt in place of the dead man who had just been removed, and as if to sanctify the worldliness of the place, they had laid a large black crucifix bearing its pale corpse of yellow ivory with its arms outstretched in agony.*

The naval officer, writing on 5 October, took his usual practical view of events.

The enemy lines are bristling with defensive works; they seem to want to reduce us by a severe blockade. We make ourselves a party to these tactics by only disturbing them with anodine reconnaissances, which do not even tell us about their position and their real strength . . .

We do not lack bold and skilful men. Do we lack the knowledge of the place? One cannot believe it, and the government must no doubt be constantly informed of what the enemy is doing. And yet I have already seen many people turned away who could have given useful information, and one often has a great deal of trouble in convincing our generals of things which are happening before their eyes. I am afraid that political preoccupations are absorbing the Governor of Paris too much. He should be more often in the forts and not so often at the Hôtel-de-Ville. Today the military side of our situation is more important than all the rest.*

Alphonse Daudet was to agree.

We mustn't seek the true history of this siege in papers or in books; we must seek it at the Ministry of War. It was there that they fought the great battle of Paris. It was there, against the quill-drivers of the military bureaucracy, that all individual efforts, all goodwill, all ardent enthusiasm, all noble ideas for the defence of Paris were wrecked.†

The bureaucrats were obstructionist; the Government was weak. On 5 October Mme Quinet saw fresh vegetables in the market. The marauders had brought them back to Paris. 'But is it wise', she asked, 'to allow this crowd of people to scatter in the fields, beyond the advance-posts, and to give the Prussians the chance of entering in pursuit? People are calling for the requisitioning of food; the Government doesn't dare to impose it . . . Material life threatens to become impossible.'‡

The only hope remained a relieving army from the provinces; and Edgar Quinet, the politician, made an appeal to the provinces in which, reported Bowles,

he points out that they are required by law to organize their Mobiles and National Guards, and to make a levy *en masse* of all the men there are left; in short, that they are bound to bring at least 700,000 troops to the succour of the capital. That, no doubt, is so. But what if they will not come? It is hardly possible to believe it, and yet I am assured that the provinces are doing practically nothing. Meantime the Parisians are vapouring and throwing flowers, and casting the statue of Strasbourg in bronze; and between these France is on the point of perishing as a nation.*

It was Léon Gambetta, the Minister of the Interior, who determined to organize the provinces. On 7 October, wandering down the boulevard de Clichy, Victor Hugo caught sight of a balloon at the end of a street leading into Montmartre.

I went there. There was quite a crowd round a big square space, walled in by the perpendicular cliffs of Montmartre. In this space were three blown-up balloons, big, middling, and small. The big one was yellow, the middling one was white, and the little one was ribbed red and yellow.

They were whispering in the crowd: '*Gambetta's going to leave!*' In fact, in a thick overcoat, under an otter-fur cap, near the yellow balloon, in a group of men, I caught sight of Gambetta. He sat down on the pavement and put on fur-lined boots. He had a leather bag slung across him. He took it off, got into the balloon, and a young man, the aeronaut, tied the bag to the rigging, above Gambetta's head.

It was half-past ten. It was a fine day. A slight south wind. A gentle autumn sun. Suddenly the yellow balloon rose up with three men, Gambetta among them. Then the white balloon, with three men, too, one of whom was waving a tricolour flag. Under Gambetta's balloon there hung a tricolour pennant. There were cries of 'Vive la République!'†

Gambetta left by balloon this morning [explained the usual naval officer] to organize the resistance in the provinces. No doubt it is useful for France to know what is happening in Paris, and to be informed about the capital; no doubt it is useful for the whole country to be rallied in one action against the invaders; but, above all things, Paris must know how to give an example of courage and patience, it

Gambetta leaving Paris by balloon

Transcribing a despatch sent by pigeon mail

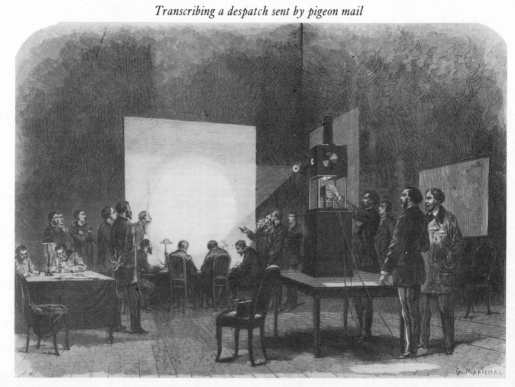

must not be too anxious about the arrival of the relieving armies. Alone at the breach, it must fight the first fights, and, without weakening, it must uphold the republican colours which it was the first to unfurl. Paris can save everything, though it is accused of compromising everything! By its resistance, it can give the provinces time to organize themselves for the struggle; by its inner calm, it can reassure those spirits which are alarmed by republican memories, and deceive the waiting enemy, who is watching its discords. But let it not forget that it has done nothing yet, and that France and Europe are waiting for its first efforts in order to measure its greatness!*

At half-past four that afternoon, Gambetta landed near Montdidier. He joined the Republican Delegation at Tours; and, within forty-eight hours of his arrival, he had added to his functions those of Minister of War.

7 October

Paris [wrote Labouchère] would hardly be recognised under its present aspect by those citizens of the Far West who are in the habit of regarding it as a place where good Americans go when they die. In the garden of the Tuileries, where *bonnes* used to flirt with guardsmen, there is an artillery camp. The guns, the pickets of horses, the tents, the camp-fires, and the soldiers in their shirt-sleeves, have a picturesque effect under the great trees. On the Place de la Concorde from morning to evening there is a mob discussing things in general, and watching the regiments as they defile with their crowns before the statue of Strasburg. In the morning the guns of the forts can be heard heavily booming; but the sound has now lost its novelty, and no one pays more attention to it than the miller to the wheel of his mill. In the Champs-Élysées there are no private carriages, and few persons sitting on the chairs. The Palais de l'Industrie is the central ambulance; the Cirque de l'Impératrice a barrack. All the cafés chantants are closed. Some few youthful votaries of pleasure still patronise the merry-go-rounds; but their business is not a lucrative one. Along the quays by the river side there are cavalry and infantry regiments with the tentes d'abri. The Champ de Mars is a camp. In most of the squares there are sheep and oxen. On the outer Boulevards lines of huts have been built for the Mobiles, and similar huts are being erected along the Rue des Remparts for the Nationaux on duty. Everywhere there are squads of Nationaux, some learning the goose-step, others practising skirmishing between the carts and fiacres, others levelling their guns and snapping them off at imaginary Prussians. The omnibuses are crowded; but I fear greatly that their horses will be far from tender when we eat them. The cabbies, once so haughty and insolent, are humble and conciliatory, for Brutus and Scaevola have taught them manners, and usually pay their fares in patriotic speeches. At the Arc de Triomphe, at the Trocadéro, and at Passy, near the Point du Jour, there are always crowds trying to see the Prussians on the distant hills, and in the Avenue de l'Impératrice (now the Avenue Uhrich), there are always numerous admirers of Mont Valérien gazing silently upon the object of their worship. In the Faubourg St Antoine workmen are lounging about doing nothing, and watching others drilling. In the outer faubourgs much the same thing goes on, except when barricades are being built. Round each of these there is always a crowd of men and women, apparently expecting the enemy to assault them every moment. At the different gates of the town there are companies of Mobiles and National Guards, who sternly repel every civilian who seeks to get through them. On an average of every ten minutes, no matter where one is, one meets either a battalion of Nationaux or Mobiles, marching somewhere.*

'Dimanche 9 octobre,' continued Edwin Child. 'Playing cards, dominoes, "bouchon" etc. etc., anything to murder time. However on Saturday with the consent of Mr Louppe Albert and I joined the "Garde Civique" – a corps formed for the keeping of the peace, half military half municipal, arresting fuyards, assisting firemen, superintending the closing of the Cafés etc. etc. By this means we hope to employ ourselves usefully instead of sleeping. Wet chiefly.'†

Two days later M. de Vineuil wrote to his wife, who was in the country:

.. And now it seems that the Prussians have renounced any idea of a surprise attack. They are establishing themselves in their positions, we are fortifying ourselves in ours, and as Paris is already very nearly impregnable, there are hardly more than two possibilities to consider: either liberation by Bazaine or surrender through famine . . .

We officers talk a lot about what the provincial armies will be, and what sort of armament they have. I am one of those who attach less importance to the value of the equipment than to that of the man who uses it . . . The determination to fight would make a soldier of any man; but will our peasants have this clear determination? They would need time to understand what the national disaster demands of them, and it is precisely time which is lacking.*

12 October

For my part [confessed the Besieged Resident] I have given up placing the least faith in anything I hear or read. As for the newspapers they give currency to the most incredible stories, and they affect not only to relate every shot that has been fired, but the precise damage which it has done to the enemy, and the number of men which it has killed and wounded. They have already slain and taken prisoner a far greater number of Prussians than, on any fair calculation, there could have been in the besieging army at the commencement of the siege. Since the commencement of the war the Government, the journalists, the generals, and the gossips have been engaged apparently in a contest to test the limits of human credulity. Under the Republic the game is still merrily kept up, and although the German armies are but a few miles off, we are daily treated to as many falsehoods respecting what goes on at the front as when they were at Sedan, or huddled together in those apocryphal quarries of Jaucourt. 'I saw it in a newspaper,' or 'I was told it by an eye-witness,' is still considered conclusive evidence of the truth of no matter what fact. Today, I nearly had a dispute with a stout party, who sat near me as I was breakfasting in a café, because I ventured, in the mildest and most hesitating manner, to question the fact that an army of 250,000 men was at Rouen, and would in the course of this week attack the Prussians at Versailles. 'It is here, sir,' he said, indignantly pointing to his news-paper; 'a peasant worthy of belief has brought this news to the Editor; are we to believe no one?' There were a dozen persons breakfasting at the same time, and I was the only one who did not implicitly believe in the existence of this army. This diseased state of mind arises mainly, I presume, from excessive vanity. No Parisian is able to believe anything which displeases him, and he is unable not to believe any-thing which flatters his *amour propre*. He starts in life with a series of delusions, which all he has read and heard until now have confirmed. No journal dares to tell the truth, for if it did its circulation would fall to nothing. No Parisian, even if by an effort he could realise to himself the actual condition of his country, would dare to communi-cate his opinion to his neighbour, for he would be regarded as a traitor and a liar. The Bostonians believe that Boston is the 'hub of the universe,' and the Parisian is under the impression that his city is a species of sacred Ark, which it is sacrilege to touch. To bombard London or Berlin would be an unfortunate necessity of war, but to fire a shot into Paris is desecration.*

Next day, however, 13 October, there occurred one of those savage, wanton acts of destruction of which there were to be so many in the days of the Commune. The château of Saint-Cloud had been bought by Louis XIV for his brother, Monsieur; for some two centuries it had been a part of French history. Since 1852 it had been the favourite palace of Napoleon III; and from Saint-Cloud, less than three months earlier, he had left to join the Army of the Rhine. Perhaps this was why the destruction of the palace caused no appreciable regret in Paris. Perhaps this was one reason why the French destroyed it themselves.†

The Germans [wrote Edmund Ollier, in his *History of the War*] accused the French of having shelled the palace without any provocation, whereas they themselves had spared it. The palace was doubtless fired because it was held to be a vantage-post to the enemy; and possibly some of those in power may have felt a certain satisfaction in shattering a building long associated with the traditions of Royalty and Imperialism. The work of destruction was effected by the fort of Mont-Valérien, about two miles and a half distant. At one pm the garrison began throwing grenades at the palace. Shortly afterwards a shell fell on the right wing, and a slight smoke was seen to rise into the air. Perceiving that the edifice was on fire, the Prussian officers ordered their men to save the furniture, books, paintings, and historical relics contained in those memorable walls; but the bombardment being continued, and the flames bursting out on all sides, very little was preserved. Such objects as could be hastily snatched from the flames were temporarily deposited in one of the alleys of trees at the back of the palace, and a few days later were removed to better quarters; among these was the table on which the Emperor had signed the declaration of war three months before. The flames burnt furiously all day; a brisk wind fanned the fire, and, as evening darkened, the Parisians, looking west, saw the horizon blood-red, with great hovering shadows of smoke. Against the scarlet glare, the long lines of statues on the façade of the palace seemed to stand out blackly, while the numerous windows spouting forth flames showed how thoroughly the work had been performed. The destruction was complete. By the morning nothing remained but a few smouldering walls . . . The French lost a portion of their history in losing Saint-Cloud; and the injury is all the more lamentable in that it was committed by themselves.*

Some months later, a French observer visited Saint-Cloud:

The château is like a décor in broad daylight, all the windows are open, without sash frames or panes, from one façade to the other; you can see the sky through it; the roof is demolished, not a yard of wall which has not been struck by a bullet. The cannon of Mont-Valérien set about this white façade with fury; one shot here, another there, then another, and another! The shells broke the wall, went through the empty galleries, came out through the opposite façade, smashed the sculptures into splinters, and mutilated the white marble statues lined up on their plinths in the garden, cutting off the head of one, smashing the finger of another, breaking the leg of a third, making new statues into antiques. The light iron bridge which stretched from the palace to the summer pavilion, where the Emperor used to have *déjeuner*, has been torn up and cast down, and has fallen into the pathway, bent like a half-curled leaf. And, inside, a mass of nameless things, cornices, woodwork, partitions, roofs, so fragmented, so broken, so crushed, that you cannot make out any object or any shape. It is just pulverized stones, lumps of earth, dust and ashes! The desolation, here, is greater than anywhere one has been, the ruin matches the man who once lived here.*

In Paris itself material life was becoming increasingly impossible. Edmond de Goncourt had recently collected a card for meat rationing. It was a piece of blue paper, 'a typographical curiosity for times to come and for the Goncourts of the future. It gives me the right, for myself and my servant, to buy two rations of raw meat every day, or four portions of food prepared in the municipal canteens.'† Butter was scarce, as well as meat, and there were citizens who tried to exploit the situation. The Press announced that

some merchants have not hesitated to sell for human consumption fats which have not been purified and are therefore unsuited for the purpose for which they are sold. Others sell as lard a mixture of various fats, and even solidified coconut oils, which are generally used in the scent industry.

Although these products, inferior in quality to the ones for which they are sold, are not harmful to health, it is useful to remind tradesmen that the law does not only punish the sale of unwholesome foods, but that it makes liable to correctional prosecution, which can bring fines, imprisonment and publication of sentence, the individual who deceives *as to the nature* of merchandise or sells *falsified* provisions.*

A biscuit manufacturer is said to have made a colossal fortune, simply by not making his usual merchandise. 'When the siege began, he had a stock of more than five thousand preserved eggs, which, on an average, had cost him less than a sou apiece. Now we paid up to 2 fr. 25 centimes each for eggs. Just calculate.'†

On 18 October, Bismarck, 'the Chief,' breakfasted with his staff and remarked that he was very fond of hard-boiled eggs: 'that now he could only manage three, but the time was when he could make away with eleven.'‡

The best German account of the siege is perhaps a small book, *Before Paris, 1870–1871*. It contains the letters of a young Berlin manufacturer, now an officer in the Prussian Garde Landwehr: letters addressed, improbably, to the editor of the *Scotsman*. The first was written from Champlan on 20 October.

The place where we are quartered today . . . is a favourite summer and Sunday sojourn of the Parisians, which I well recollect from former visits to Paris. We are living in charming little villas or in enormous *cafés*; but there was never a soul to bid us welcome [*sic*]. A deep silence, the silence of death, reigned around us, as we entered the place. We are sleeping under rich silk canopies, and we dine – at the officers' mess – off the most delicate Sèvres china, only, unfortunately, our dinners issue from the hands of our soldier-servants, few of whom have made any gastronomic studies, and the bill of fare is humble, not to say monotonous, consisting one day of bacon and potatoes, and the next of potatoes and bacon. To make up for this, we certainly get splendid fruit by way of dessert – pears and apples the like of which, I verily believe, only grow in the vicinity of Paris . . .

From the highest point here you can survey the immeasurable array of the houses of Paris; and any one who knows this most gloriously beautiful city, this town of towns, can easily 'spot', with an average field-glass, the towers of *Notre-Dame*, and of the *Dôme des Invalides*. Is the day still distant when, in the joyfulness of victory, we shall march along the Boulevards? As I write, the roar of cannon is becoming so loud and fierce, that we may dismiss any hopes of speedy peace as devoid of foundation 'until further notice'.*

Gustave Flaubert to Princess Mathilde:

Croisset,
Sunday, 23 October 1870

... If Bazaine frees himself and Bourbaki joins him, while the army of the Loire is marching to Paris, all is not lost, because the Parisians will make a mass sortie which will, I have no doubt, be terrible. We have enough men and we shall soon have enough artillery; but what we lack are leaders, it's a commander. Oh for a man! A man! Just one! A good mind to save us. As for the provinces, I consider them as lost. The Prussians can spread out indefinitely, but as long as Paris isn't taken France is still alive ...

How they hate us! And how they envy us, those cannibals! Do you know that they take pleasure in destroying works of art, and luxuries, when they find them? Their dream is to destroy Paris, because Paris is beautiful.†

On 27 October, Thomas Gibson Bowles gave an English assessment of the situation.

I am beginning now to think that the defence of Paris will figure in history rather as an absurd caricature than the serious effort of serious men ...

Those who are actually on the spot, and competent to appreciate the situation, and observe what is actually being done, must testify that, in presence of the danger that menaces them, the Parisians have hitherto been so utterly trivial that it has become quite sickening to put their words side by side with their acts. They will die on the ramparts. They will bury themselves beneath the ruins of Paris. They will astonish the world, we are told every day, and yet here they still sit

The French artillery at Mont Valérien

The Garde Nationale on the ramparts

with folded arms, 500,000 men with rifles and bayonets in their hands, not daring to strike a blow. Even their purely defensive works are ridiculous. They make holes and fill them with spikes; sow their ramparts with nails, points upwards, and propose even to cover them with broken glass, as if the Prussians were so many cats. But it is only a small number who even do so much as this; the rest simply go on eating and drinking as usual . . .

Seeing Paris so utterly enervated and futile, it is not wonderful that the provinces will not move. It is pretty well established that up to this time they have done nothing whatever; and as the defence of Paris is solely of use, if at all, to give the provinces time to rise, it is clear that if no help is to come from them peace had better be made at once, and at any price.*

Théophile Gautier to Carlotta Grisi:

Paris, 4th letter by balloon
31 October 1870

My dear Carlotta,

I write to you none too hopeful that my letter will reach you. The weather is appalling, very much against the departure of balloons: furious wind, and unceasing rain. All the same I shall try to write, and perhaps this scrap of paper will get through to you. The situation is as grievous as it can be. We heard tonight of the surrender of Metz which had been left unaided. Bazaine is a prisoner with sixty thousand men, and the Prussian army he held in check before Metz is now free and will fall on us again. We captured Le Bourget the day before yesterday; the enemy recaptured it this morning . . . I don't think we shall be freed between now and 4 November. My health, and my sisters' health, is good, despite the fantastic food in which we indulge. We are eating horse, donkey, macaroni without butter or cheese; we shall soon be down to rats and mice. The horse is excellent, but the donkey is a real delicacy. There is nothing less true than the phrase: 'Tough as a donkey.' The plan seems to be to get us through famine, for there has been no serious attack. The Prussians do not even answer the fire from our forts, and it's all limited to skirmishes in the suburbs with people going in search of potatoes. I am writing some articles called *Voyages dans Paris* for the *Officiel*; they are having a great success and they will make a strange enough book after the Siege. There is nothing more melancholy than Paris at this moment. The cafés shut at half-past ten; the shops don't even open during the day. We're rationed for gas as we are for meat. We only light one jet in four and the sight of these dark streets, where a rare passer-by brushes against the walls and we do not hear the sound of a single carriage, is really not calculated to enliven us. But either we bury ourselves beneath the ruins of Paris or we die of hunger if we cannot fight our way out. The resolution is very firmly made.*

III *NOVEMBER 1870*

On 1 November, the anonymous subaltern in the Prussian Landwehr wrote another letter to the *Scotsman*. The previous day his regiment had been reviewed by King William at Versailles.

The King, with the white cross of the Landwehr fixed to his helmet, and 'his fair-haired hero son', to use the stereotype phrase of a certain reporter, by his side, rode up to each company and addressed them... Then we passed on, column by column, before the valiant old man, whose face was beaming with benevolence and joyousness.

We are now [reported the officer] quartered at Marly, a gloriously beautiful place ... Right before us lies the Fort du Mont Valérien, the proudest fort of Paris, standing out clearly and boldly against the autumnal tints of the Bois de Boulogne ...

We ... are quartered in a mansion built in the Versailles style, and belonging to M. Sardou, the well-known author. The elegance and luxury which I found displayed within its walls beggars description... My bedroom is hung with rich grey silk – canopied bedstead, and furniture generally are of yellow damask. There are splendid mirrors, let into the wall, set in a framework, as it were, of some delicately-beautiful, ethereal, diaphanous, snow-white stuff; elaborate marble mantelpieces, one holding the marble bust *de la reina castissima*, Isabella, ex-Queen of Spain, the other, that of the beautiful Empress of the French – the latter bust being a genuine work of art, wrought by a master's hand. Thus much for my bedroom; pass we now into the dressing-room – momentarily allotted to me, a lieutenant in a Prussian Landwehr regiment; and behold rich furniture in blue silk, covered with delicate tulle (or some such humbug), dressing-tables laden with bottles and boxes of the costliest scents, with *poudre de riz*, with preparations and utensils innumerable, and positively bewildering. The owners must have fled precipitately, leaving everything behind them ...

But oh! what is the use to us of such rooms, such luxurious couches and beds? A heavy booming is ever and anon heard as coming from Mont Valérien, and as yet we have not passed a single night in beautiful Marly without having been summoned to arms. That, of course, is sure to be the case anywhere and everywhere around Paris ... O hang it! there goes the alarm-drum even as I write. So I'm off!*

The Germans were restive. So, too, were the inhabitants of the beleaguered capital. John O'Shea confessed:

I had lived in Paris for months without desire to cross the gates; but, somehow or other, the moment it was impossible to get out I felt like the starling in *The Sentimental Journey*. What would I not have given in reason for a ramble through the forest of St Germain, or a pull on the river at Asnières? The city was large enough in all conscience, yet the sense of restraint was oppressive. There was one philosopher who took things easily – a very old soldier at the Invalides. He was a violinist and an angler, and went down daily, when he was tired of fiddling, to fish by the viaduct at Auteuil. Yet he had his grievance: the cannonade hindered the gudgeon from biting.†

The Oxford Graduate, like O'Shea, felt an overwhelming sense of imprisonment:

What a comfort that the Bois de Boulogne remains open, and that one can escape there from this pent-up, stifling Bedlam which the world calls Paris ...

True, I see no fashionable equipages on the drive round the lakes, no *pur-sangs* of Albion, no powder, no paint, no golden chignons that changed in hue with the dye of Cora's hair; they are gone, they are vanished, and gone with them the glory of Imperial days. This time next year the golden chignons may revive, and under the auspicious reign of His Majesty Louis-Philippe the Second, . . . the Bois de Boulogne, this cynical old jade of a bois, will revive in all its cynical voluptuousness ... Just now I heard a sound of wheels, and I saw a dog-cart with an intrepid *élégante* sitting on the box: about her person and her toilette lingered some faint subdued reminiscence of the days

of chignon and powder; she was 'in mourning for her country' –
mourning befitted the delicate Parisian pallor of her complexion, and
instead of a lap-dog she carried an opera-glass, armed with which
she had come out . . . to satisfy her curiosity by a peep at the Morte-
mart battery or the cascade near Longchamp, at the spots 'where the
enemy might be'.*

Some Parisians who remained in the beleaguered city were oppressed
not only by the Siege, but by the thoughts of the homes which they
had been compelled to leave. Théophile Gautier had left his suburban
house at Neuilly for a lodging in the rue de Beaune, in the heart of
Paris. After a few weeks, he felt impelled, whatever the risk, to pay
a visit to the rue de Longchamp. The desire took hold of him with
irresistible intensity. In one of the most poignant chapters in *Tableaux
de Siège* he described his expedition.

We could no longer read or write; our pen stopped in the middle of
a line, waiting for the spirit to guide it, but the spirit was elsewhere.
We had absolutely sworn not to leave the city until the moment of
triumph, when the enemy had been driven away. We had to give in
and perjure ourselves. We could not bear it any more. And so we set
off with our usual companion on expeditions.

As we passed the Arc de Triomphe, we noticed that they had finally
boarded up the bas-reliefs on the two façades. They had at first
thought of keeping Rude's masterpiece, *Le Départ des Volontaires*,
and Cortot's group – which are less exposed, however, since they are
facing towards Paris. It was a good precaution when all is said, though
the scar of a bullet or shell does not spoil a heroic piece of sculpture.

In front of the imposing edifice, on the side of the avenue de la
Grande-Armée, there is always a crowd, a kind of open-air club which
discusses the questions of the day, and exchanges the real or invented
news. One can learn on the spot how legends are formed: how public
imagination adds, in all sincerity, to actual facts the element of poetry
it needs. So it is that, from the various accounts enlarged or fused

into one, there gradually emerges the *romancero* of the ramparts. The exploits of the militia and the sharpshooters, recalled with enthusiasm by the people, remind one of the feats of Chingachgook and of Falcon-Eye in pursuit of the Mingos.

Barricades, very carefully erected, cut across the road two or three times between the Arc de Triomphe and the barrier; yet as far as that the aspect of the place has not really changed. But when you have crossed the drawbridge of the rampart, and the defences which are concentrated at this point, you would think yourself in an unknown land, because the place has so changed its appearance. The military zone of the fortifications, completely demolished and razed to the ground, offers perspectives never seen before. On the right, as you come out of Paris, you see a commemorative chapel; it was built to mark the spot where the Duc d'Orléans died, on the chemin de la Révolte. No doubt it earned grace as an historic monument; besides, its low and tomblike form did not demand imperiously that it was sacrificed. One used to admire some magnificent stained-glass windows there, based on cartoons by Ingres; no doubt they have been stored away for safety. On the other side, M. Gellé's factory used to be remarkable for its high pink brick chimney and the suave fragrance of perfumery which it spread around; the factory has been demolished, and the neighbouring houses have suffered the same fate as far as the Porte Maillot road.

This demolition allows one to see the whole façade of the restaurant Gillet. There are no revelries there any more, the banquets have been stopped, and, coming home from the Bois, you no longer see a couple get out of their carriage and slip away quickly and furtively up the stairs to the private rooms to have an intimate dinner. The stoves, which were once always flaming, are now cold. But there is quite as much animation in front of the main entrance. General Ducrot has established his headquarters at Gillet's, and there is a constant movement of orderlies, troopers, soldiers and people coming to get permits, because you cannot go beyond the pont de Neuilly without permission.

When we went home to the rue de Longchamp, we often used to take the avenue Maillot; it goes along the edge of the Bois de Boulogne, from which it is divided by a rather deep ditch. In the ordinary way it is a very pleasant road. On one side you have the Bois and, on the other, a row of elegant houses with little gardens in front of them. The road itself is planted with chestnut trees, but we shall come back to that in a moment.

When we had turned the corner by the restaurant, an unknown landscape suddenly unfurled before our eyes. We were absolutely amazed. As far as we could see, there stretched a vast zone which was bristling with shafts like truncated columns. It recalled one of those Oriental cemeteries where every tomb is marked by a marble post; save for the gigantic cypresses, it was the very image of the Field of the Dead at Eyoub or Scutari. Yet we were not in Constantinople, but at the Porte Maillot. Vague trails of bluish smoke, light trails of vapour crept along the ground and were borne away by the wind. They helped to intensify the illusion. These columns were not Turkish tombs, but the tree-trunks of the poor Bois de Boulogne, which had been felled three feet from the ground. This immense felling of trees gave a clear and distant view of buildings usually hidden behind the leaves: buildings seemed irregular blocks on the plain which had been stripped bare. It was a heartrending desolation, but not without its beauty. This severe horizon would have charmed an artist.

The work of felling continued, and here and there a tree fell with a dull groan, and we should not like to swear that it was always a strategic sacrifice and that the woodcutters always had the powers of military genius. Haggard old women constantly passed by, more horrific than the sibyl of Panzoust, of whom one would only have known that she breathed. They made their way under enormous armfuls of wood, and the branches covered them behind like a carapace and made them look like turtles rearing up on their hind legs. A little girl of twelve or thirteen was running with a tree-trunk four or five feet long on her shoulder. But there are faggots and faggots, as Sganarelle says, and siege faggots are substantial.

The *hôtels*, villas, cottages, in Elizabethan, Renaissance and Flem-
ish style, which border the avenue Maillot, are nearly all abandoned,
and serve as billets for the militia, as attested by the shirts and
trousers hanging from the windows. Among these delightful houses,
there was one which pleased us more than all the rest, one in which
we liked to imagine scenes of happiness. It seemed to us that they
must be happy in this *palazzino*, sheltered behind a curtain of ivy.
Through a gap in the foliage we admired the white stone pillars, the
flight of smooth stone steps, the happy mixture of coloured bricks,
the balcony overflowing with flowers, the blinds which remained
discreetly lowered and scattered with a few painted birds. The house
was still there, but its expression was different. It had a weary,
melancholy air.

We had to leave the avenue Maillot, for it was obstructed by barricades which became more formidable still as one approached the
avenue de Madrid. We reached the avenue de Longchamp by almost
deserted side-roads, where militia came and went, and gunners cooked
their pittance with brushwood and kindling wood picked up in the
wasteland.

The barking of an occasional dog disturbed and surprised by our
passing was all that broke the silence. From time to time there rang
out a shot destined for a sparrow – and in the distance one heard the
rolls of a school of drummers.

At last we stood in front of our house. We had not been sure if we
should find the remotest trace of it. On the outside, nothing had
changed. The head of the Victory of the Parthenon (M. de Laborde
brought the marble back from Athens) figures, cast in plaster, on a
classical red background, in a circular niche, on our studio wall. It
was still in place: the triumphant sister of the Venus de Milo, the
superb power of form, *vis superba formae*, the immortal ideal of
beauty, tutelary genius of the humble dwelling. A window was open,
as if the house still sheltered its old inhabitants. That seemed a good
omen to us. We rang. The gardener came and opened the door.
Touched to the heart, we entered this habitation, as small as that

of Socrates, this house which had not been hard to fill with friends.

When you enter a dwelling which has been deserted for a long while, you always seem to be disturbing someone. Invisible guests have settled there during your absence, and they retreat before you. As you open doors, you seem to see the last fold of their vanishing robes floating on the threshold. Solitude and abandonment have done something mysterious, something which you are interrupting. At the sight of you, the whispering spirits are silent, the spider ceases to spin its rose-window. Deep silence falls and, in the empty rooms, the echo of your steps has strange sonorities. There had not been the slightest damage. And nobody had been there since we left. The poet's modest refuge had been respected.

On our bedroom mantelpiece a volume of Alfred de Musset still lay open at the abandoned page. On the wall there hung the copy of a head by Ricard, begun by our dear daughter. Alas, she is so far away ... And she will not read this article. An open bottle of scent evaporated on her white marble dressing-table, and it spread its faint and gentle perfume in her little virginal room.

We went up to the studio which we were arranging for long labours which perhaps will never end. There was only the roof to be put in place, and we thought of that sombre aphorism of Oriental wisdom: 'When the house is finished, death comes in.' Death or disaster. Deep melancholy took possession of us as we looked at these places where we have loved, where we have suffered, where we have borne life as it is, a mixture of good and ill, with more ill than good, the place where they have flowed away, the days which will return no more, the place which was visited by many whom we loved, many who have set out on the final journey. We felt there, in our humble way, something like the sadness of Olympio ...

It was getting late, and the gates of Paris now shut at five o'clock. Before we left our dear abandoned house, we went and took a turn in the garden. The evening mist had begun to rise and leave a bluish haze at the ends of the paths. The wind stirred the wet leaves, the bare trees trembled and shivered as if they were cold. Some dahlias were withering in the flower-beds, and an old familiar blackbird, booted with yellow, suddenly took off before our feet, flapping his wings as if he wanted to greet us. Mont-Valérien sent two formidable cannon-shots to bid good-night to the Prussian redoubts; they did not really seem to frighten the bird, which was used to such commotion.

It is the blackbird which nests every spring in the old ivy, a green drapery cast over the wall, and whistles with a mocking air as he passes by our window, as if he were reading what we were writing.*

Flaubert and countless others had hoped that Marshal Bazaine would break out of Metz and come to relieve the beleaguered capital. But Marshal Bazaine, who 'smoked by day and played billiards by night,' had made no attempt to break out of Metz. On 29 October, after seventy days of siege, he had surrendered the starving city to the enemy. Then he had ridden into captivity. When the news reached Tours, Gambetta had had Bazaine proclaimed a traitor. On 31 October, the Government in Paris had been obliged to announce that Metz had fallen.

The gloom increased; on 4 November M. de Vineuil confessed to his wife:

The fall of Metz weighs on us. This misfortune, added to the silence of the provinces, has killed the martial spirit among us. We feel condemned, we tell each other that it is futile and therefore criminal to prolong the struggle, since the provincial armies are not in a state to take part in it. General Trochu is reported to have said: 'The defence of Paris can only be heroic madness.' I don't know how authentic that is, but it is none the less true that this declaration . . . has now assumed all the proportions of a prophecy.†

If, as I hear [added Whitehurst next day], fresh meat will only hold out a fortnight, and the dry supplies are not very great (there is plenty of bread-stuff and wine), we must make peace or fight an awful battle before Christmas; and indeed, as the troops would on lower rations be getting weaker every day, I should think Trochu would attack (if he were not attacked himself) at once.*

On 10 November, Henri Dabot recorded that rats were being sold at Les Halles at 25 centimes each. Wickham Hoffman, of the American Legation, added that 'dogs sold from 80 cents up, according to size and fat. There was a refinement in rats. They were known as the brewery rat and the sewer rat. The brewery rat was naturally the most delicate titbit.'†

It is now eight weeks [continued Bowles] since we began to run up and down in this great city, like Sterne's starling crying, 'I can't get out! I can't get out!' At first it was novel, and, therefore, entertaining. The cage was a large one, and as we beat about the bars we thought it vastly fine to be in such an incredible situation, and we admired ourselves hugely – I speak as a Parisian – and called loudly upon the world at large to admire us too . . .

Well, if the truth be told, we don't admire ourselves nearly as much now. The fact is that we are getting bored. *Anything* that lasts two months becomes a nuisance, I don't care what it is; and we are beginning to want something new – even if it were Peace . . . Let us get out of Paris, and renew our acquaintance with fresh butter and daily news.‡

The inhabitants of Paris were eagerly gazing out; the Prussians were eagerly gazing in. On 13 November, this time from Argenteuil, the subaltern in the Garde Landwehr reported:

There is a very pretty modern church here . . . We have established an observatory on the top thereof, and thence you can see the be-leaguered city so well that you might fancy a short and harmless stroll would take you to the *Arc de Triomphe* – the chiselled figures on it we can trace most minutely with a good field-glass. There is a busy life going on inside. The engine of the railway round the city is dashing to and fro; smoke issues from all the chimneys; and certain experts stoutly maintain they can make out a steady, regularly continued noise as of huge iron hammers, working by day and working by night. The French trumpets, too, are being sounded frequently, with a sound marvellously like our Prussian artillery signals, and with their bright music mingle the deeper voices of the drums. Trochu, it is clear, is drilling his battalions of the Garde Nationale, and making a great deal more noise than the beleaguering army, the silence in whose ranks contrasts strangely with the din inside the city. It is a huge and strong ring that runs round poor Paris, and no human being is allowed to pass through our lines. Yet Paris is not cut off from all communication. Balloons come and go – they are rich in the power of invention, the French – and, in spite of our great vigilance, we frequently notice that they are holding communication with the outer world through lighted beacons and what not. We keep a smart look-out, of course, for persons signalling to the Prussians by means of lights fixed in peculiar positions, by broken arms of windmills, and the like; and if a fellow is convicted of this offence he gets short shrift – he is shot at once; such is martial law.*

Théophile Gautier to his daughter:

6th letter by Balloon post
14 November, 59th day of the siege, 1870

My dear little Estelle,

I am much afraid that my last letter didn't reach you. The Galilée balloon fell into the hands of the Prussians and I fear that the letter I sent you and the one addressed to Carlotta in which I sent my best wishes for her saint's day didn't stay at the bottom of the basket. I'm beginning all over again. What a long time it is since I saw you, dear child! The days of the siege are longer than other days, and they can count as months! One couldn't imagine a sadder or more sombre existence, and in spite of all my longing to see you I am glad to know that you are a long way away. As for danger, there is none, in the real sense of the word; the city is not seriously attacked, but it is so besieged that we shall die of hunger in a given time. In this dungeon several leagues round I don't, like Ugolino, have the resource of eating my children, since they are in Switzerland or England. There has been no butter for a long while, oil is beginning to run short, cheese is a myth and I confess that macaroni with salt and water is a poor repast. The meat ration has come down to forty grammes a day for each person and you only get your share when you have queued for three hours. I have eaten horse, donkey, mule, but there soon won't be any more. They are setting up butchers' shops . . . where they sell dog, cat, and even rats and house-sparrows. A fairly sturdy dog is worth 20 francs, half a cat 6 francs, rats and house-sparrows 50 centimes. Forgive me for all these details, but the great thing is to feed oneself. When you meet someone the first question you ask is: have you any meat? That has replaced the ordinary 'How are you?' But all this is nothing, what is heartrending is to be immured in a tomb separated from France and from the world, knowing nothing of what is happening beyond Châtillon or Saint-Denis, never receiving any answers to the letters you write, not even knowing if they arrive, not even being able at the risk of your life to rediscover the people you love. What is heartrending is to feel yourself abandoned by all the world, not to be able to send money to those who may perhaps need it, to imagine that they are ill or dead. There is no harder trial, and no deeper anguish. Think a little about us, for we love you very much . . . Two big kisses from your besieged father.

THÉOPHILE GAUTIER*

19 November

Our inactivity continues [wrote the naval officer]. Until now the weather has been favourable, now it is growing rainy as if to teach us that a chance which has been wasted does not occur again . . .

What is lacking in our leaders, alas! is belief in success, it is that faith that conquers obstacles, breaks resistance and electrifies soldiers. The discouraged language of ageing generals, who feel themselves unequal to their task, is reflected in the conversations of the officers around them; the accomplishment of military duty seems to have lost all its attraction; this very duty, as far as Paris is concerned, seems to be an annoying prejudice which they would like to cast aside . . .*

22 November

People are very depressed today [Whitehurst recorded] – it is very wet. *Figaro* has a most lachrymose article entitled 'Tomorrow', and Paris is put on salt rations. The truth is, we shall be starved out before Christmas if we do not attack successfully, and I have just heard that we must wait three weeks for the guns! My concierge also tells me that he is drilled with the old musket, which is taken away from him when the drill is over, and serves for several battalions . . .

The gas is to be cut off us all – private houses, clubs, and restaurants, after 30 November.†

23 November

Idleness and drunkenness always go together [wrote Bowles], and I suppose there never was a time when the latter vice was so common in Paris. The National Guards are drunk upon the ramparts, the workmen drunk all about the streets, and even the *cochers de fiacre* are drunk upon their boxes, to an extent that is really astonishing.‡

The best part of my time [was] occupied walking about the town to see the progress of the fortifications [recorded Edwin Child in his diary]. Each Tuesday at the Poste of the Garde Civique. Passed several days voluntarily at the Mairie Rue Drouot to help receive the reclamations regarding the rationnement of butcher's meat . . .

On the 23rd after a joking kind of question from Mr Louppe, it being almost impossible to obtain any money from him, I volunteer'd into his company of Garde Nationale de Marche, i.e. the 3rd Company of the 3rd Bataillon of which he is Sergent-Fourrier, introduced to the Captain (Gastin de Barthélemy) the same day & began my exercise the 24th received our guns the 26th & were 'rigged out' for a campaign with sack, tent, rug, boots, etc. etc. etc. etc. on the 29th. Frosty dry weather.§

'One feels bored in this siege,' added Edmond de Goncourt, 'as if it were a tragedy with no ending.'*

Wednesday evening, 23 November,
66th day of the siege

Raining until noon [noted Mr Washburne, the American Minister in Paris]. At one, it had cleared up and I went to the photographer, who complained of my looking 'too sober'. Have been laying in some canned green corn, Lima beans, canned oysters, etc. All this sort of thing is being 'gobbled up'. Nobody can tell how long we are in for it, and to what extremes we may be pushed. I first put the siege at sixty days, and here we are at sixty-six days, and no light ahead. The French seem to be getting more and more hopeful every day [*sic*]. Gambetta sends his proclamations pinned to a pigeon's tail, and tells of a great many things in the provinces, and then there is a prodigious excitement all over the city.†

Sometimes the airborne messengers fell into Prussian hands; sometimes, by chance, the wind blew them astray. On 24 November Edmund Ollier reported:

Two aeronauts, whose design was to go from Paris to Tours with sundry bags of letters, were carried northward by a contrary wind, blown over the sea by furious gales, and finally landed in a strange country, covered with snow, black with pine-forests, cruelly cold, and apparently peopled only with wolves. When at length they discovered some human beings, in the shape of woodcutters inhabiting a small cabin, it was found that their language was utterly strange to the half-frozen travellers. They were in Norway, and had come a distance of at least six hundred miles in thirteen hours.‡

25 November

Nothing new in Paris, but nothing worse [recorded Edmond Got, a *sociétaire* of the Comédie-Française]. There are certainly several armies active in the provinces, and one of them re-occupied Orleans, after a victory on the 16th.

The two million people, so unbelievably shut up here, learned this from a microscopic despatch brought in under the wing of a pigeon.*

26 November

Felix Whitehurst reported: 'They take 50 to 1 freely on the bastions that the Emperor or his family come back.'†

Théophile Gautier to Carlotta Grisi:

Letter No. 7
74th day of siege, 30 November 1870

I am writing to you to the sound of a terrible cannonade. They are making a sortie with a great many soldiers and artillery. The match is being decided at this moment and so my thoughts naturally go towards you and my poor little Estelle, whom I haven't seen for so long. I hope you are all very well over there, and dear Ernestine, too. I am well, and indeed much better than before the siege. To say we are living prosperously would be a lie: this morning I regaled myself with a rat *pâté* which wasn't bad at all. You will understand the sadness of our life. The rest of the world no longer exists for us. For nearly three months, now, we have been without news of those we love. It was time to make a violent effort to get out of such a situation; it is being made. Will it succeed? God grant it will! But they are going about it with desperate resolution and heroic fury. Everyone feels that he must conquer or perish. Ah! my poor Carlotta, it is a most lamentable year, the year 1870. What events, what catastrophes! And that without all the solace, all the sweetness of your friendship! I cannot now forget all these sinister things at the sight of you, cannot even have the resource of seeing your dear writing. I know you are thinking of me in that haven of Saint-Jean where I have spent so many charming hours; but, though I know correspondence is impossible, I feel utterly sad, and I conjure up a thousand dreams. I imagine my dear ones ill, unhappy, or, what would be worse, forgetful. A balloon is leaving tonight: will it be more fortunate than the earlier ones that were taken by the Prussians, and carried two of my letters which you therefore can't have received? I am writing to you in all haste. The news of the expedition is good; the affair is going well and perhaps the victory that has so long deserted us will return! ... Be well assured that if I do not come and see you, it is the fault of 300,000 Prussians: it would not take less than that to stop me from bringing you my good wishes on your saint's day.*

IV *DECEMBER 1870*

Night of 1–2 December

During the night [wrote Henri Dabot] I caught sight of women waiting outside the gas-works in the avenue de Choisy; they had been
there since three o'clock in the morning, and they will stay in the
same place until eight or nine o'clock, in appalling cold; they are
waiting for a little coke! . . . Poor wretches! They sit on the ground,
when they are too tired; sometimes they show their scorn of the cold
and the fatigue and sing *La Marseillaise.**

Fontenay-le-Fleury,
by Versailles,
3 December

From the Court Palace of Versailles the black-and-white flag is floating, and side by side with it, the red cross on white ground, the
emblem of the Geneva Convention. Was it by chance or design [asked
the Prussian subaltern]? In the gorgeous, lofty rooms of Louis the
Great, vainest and proudest of kings, sick men and wounded, friends
and foes, are lying quietly side by side . . .

These pictured halls of Versailles Palace which are not claimed by
the infirmary managers swarm with officers and men. Lost in amazement, the eyes of our brave fellows are held as if spellbound by the
pictures representing the glorious deeds of French arms . . . These
splendid, gallant soldiers – these proud commanders – where are
they? All, all of them beaten, and most of them prisoners at home, in
the German Fatherland! In one of the saloons . . . are the portraits,
full life-size, of Marshals MacMahon and Bazaine. A few days ago I
saw Moltke standing before these pictures. He remained a long time
there, his wonderfully deep and clear blue eyes riveted on the features
of these two generals, once so famous, whom his genius has overcome.†

5 December

The following is a list of the prices of 'luxuries' [noted Labouchère,
in Paris]. Terrines of chicken, 16f; of rabbit, 13f; . . . a goose, 45f;

one cauliflower, 3f; one cabbage, 4f; dog is 2f a lb.; a cat skinned costs 5f; a rat, 1f, if fat from the drains, 1f 50c. Almost all the animals in the Jardin des Plantes have been eaten. They have averaged about 7f a lb. Kangaroo, however, has been sold for 12f the lb. Yesterday I dined with the correspondent of a London paper. He had managed to get a large piece of moufflon, an animal which is, I believe, only found in Corsica. I can only describe it by saying that it tasted of moufflon, and nothing else . . . I do not think that I shall take up my residence in Corsica, in order habitually to feed upon it.*

Edwin Child, of the Garde civique:

7 December

Bolted into a cantine that I had discovered, & had a really delicious steak off the horse of one of the Prussian *éclaireurs* that had been killed the previous night, how I blessed the poor chap & hoped somebody else would follow in his footsteps.†

8 December

Hunger is beginning [wrote Goncourt in his *Journal*], and famine is on the horizon. And elegant Parisiennes are beginning to turn their dressing-rooms into hen-houses. People calculate and count and wonder if, with all the waste, all the scraps, all the scrapings, there will be something to eat a fortnight hence.

It isn't only food, it's lighting which is going to fail. Oil for burning is growing scarce, candles have come to an end. And, worst of all, in the current cold, we are very near the time when we shan't find any more coal or coke or wood. We are going to enter famine, coldness, darkness; and the future seems to us to promise suffering and horror the like of which no other siege has known.‡

Which of us has not stopped, on our way through the Palais-Royal, in front of Chevet's window [asked Gautier, in *Tableaux de Siège*]? It is a pleasure which the most ascetic would not deny himself. All thoughts of good fare apart, one could admire this splendid composition of victuals, like a picture by Sneyders, Weenincx or de Fyt. Roebuck were hanging outside, and brushing with black muzzles the boars' heads which were stuffed with pistachios and baring their chops in rebarbative fashion. On the white marble tables, the big salt-water fish were laid out, and gleaming with their reflections of silver and pearly rainbows; lobsters, marbled with yellow and black, waved their formidable accoutrement of claws; turtles had their clumsy frolics on the edge of the moss-rimmed basin where Chinese carp were swimming under a tinkling trickle of water. Delicate fattened pullets from Le Mans, turkeys of exceptional size, bulged out their stomachs, distended and marbled with blue by the truffles showing through their delicate skin. The grouse, the pheasants with bronzed plumage, ptarmigan from Scotland, hazel grouse from Russia, partridges with adorable little pink morocco boots, seemed to pose for the pleasure of artists as much as gourmets.

We shall not forget the pâtés de foie gras, the terrines from Nérac, the thrush pâtés from Corsica, the brochettes of ortolans and other *galanteries*, as they say in Hamburg, but how can one fail to remember those grapes from Thoméry, as blond as amber, those peaches from Montreuil, which were not the *tuppence farthing* peaches scorned by Alexandre Dumas *fils*, but genuine virgin peaches with all their bloom and all their velvet pile? How can one fail to remember those pomegranates, whose half-open rind revealed a casket of rubies; those pears so perfect that they seemed to be sculpted in Florentine alabaster to be served at the hard stone tables of the old Grand Dukes of Tuscany; that whole delightful combination of shapes and colours, that savoury Pantagruelian bouquet which was arranged with such exquisite art?

The other evening it was raining, and the need for shelter had driven us under the arcades of the Palais-Royal. Out of an old mechanical habit, we looked towards Chevet's window. Oh, surprise! Instead of the famous stock of comestibles there shone, with the crude brilliance of a pantomime setting shot with tinsel, a splendid tinsmith's shop. It was a whole construction of tin boxes, round, square, and oblong, symmetrically arranged like the basalt columns of some Fingal's Cave, illuminated where they projected with metallic light,

Queuing for rats

their gold-varnished labels gleaming. We went up. Alas! It was indeed Chevet's, but there were no more provisions – at least fresh provisions. Out of despair, they had displayed the *landsturm* of tinned food: tinned milk, bison's bosses, reindeer's tongues, tuna, American salmon, *petits pois* and even ordinary *à la mode* beef: all the provisions you take with you when you set out for the Arctic or the Antarctic Pole. The turtles had been taken away for the last mockle-turtles [*sic*] of the English who had stayed in Paris, and in the carp basin floated a little carp which really didn't look in the least as if it had come from the Rhine.

We studied it with the philosophy inspired by things set too far out of reach, and we repeated Bilboquet's wise words: 'I'll come back next week.'

However, in front of another window a crowd had assembled in an attitude of deep admiration. We went up, and at first we saw nothing but a gen-seng root. Its main parts were writhing like the legs of Cornelius, the mandragora turned into a Field-Marshal in the tale by Achim d'Arnim. There were also two or three pots of preserved Chinese ginger covered with bamboo wickerwork. It was not these which excited the respectful amazement of the crowd, it was a lump of fresh butter, about half a kilogram, triumphantly set out on a plate. Never was the yellow block displayed by the lottery for the gold ingot contemplated with eyes more admiring, more shining with desire, more phosphorescent with covetousness. These burning glances were mingled with glowing tenderness, with memories of happier times . . .

People have often acclaimed the courage, the abnegation, the patriotism of Paris . . . One word is enough – Paris does without butter!*

Henri Dabot:

Horse hasn't been very scarce since the battle of Champigny, where more than 1500 horses were killed, so it is said; I don't know about this; but what I do know is that for the past few days I have regaled myself at Duval's on horse cooked as beef; now it is finished, no more

steeds to devour; I am eating salt beef and salt mutton; I don't like
the mutton very much: I am only eating it in order to preserve a
husband for my wife and a father for my children. My friend J—
is terrified of eating so much salt meat. He is obsessed with a fear of
scurvy. He is feeling his jaws every minute, and moistening them
with honey of roses.

Paris is covered with sparkling white snow; it seems to be wrapped
in its shroud!*

Mme Edmond Adam, wife of the politician, wrote to her daughter:

11 December

A wretched day! It is cold indoors, wood is scarce, we're freezing,
it is very slippery in the streets. The works are not progressing on
the plain of Avron, one can't shift, stir or dig the hardened soil . . .

The soldiers are dying of cold in the trenches, at the outposts, for
want of clothes. We are collecting flannel shirts, socks and waistbands
for them. The commissariat would rather die than adjust itself to
circumstances and modify its rules; it gives our soldiers new clothes
only once a year. They've been under fire for six weeks, they've been
in the rain for three months, they have been sent among the barbed
wire in gratitude. What does it matter? The commissariat has the
idea that the rags of soldiers do as much honour to the French army
as the gleaming gold lace of the generals.

I have seen almost naked soldiers at the outposts, and others arrive
in our hospitals with their trousers and their tunics in rags.†

Wickham Hoffman, of the American Legation:

11 December

I breakfasted in December with a French general, who commanded
one of the outposts. We had beef, eggs, ham, etc., and, from what I
heard, I should say that he and his staff breakfasted as well every day.
These noonday breakfasts, by the way, ruined the French army. I
reached my general's headquarters at half-past eleven. He and one
of his staff were smoking cigars and drinking absinthe. At twelve we
breakfasted bountifully, as I have said, and with champagne, and

other wines, followed by coffee, brandy, and more cigars. This was an outpost in presence of the enemy. Had he attacked, what would the general and his staff have been worth? They were very far from being intoxicated, but certainly their heads were not clear, or their judgments sound.*

Felix Whitehurst:

12 December

I thought I had never seen any body of men . . . so utterly uncomfortable as the National Guards at drill today; and their dress, I cannot say uniform, was a motley spectacle. For instance, one man had on I presume his regimentals, then shoes and black cloth gaiters, a brown great-coat, and a cotton pocket-handkerchief tied over his képi; add to this, spectacles and a cigar.†

Mme Edgar Quinet:

13 December

What can one say of the situation, which is still the same? The days resemble one another, dismal, deadened, petrified, and they do not bring any change. No armies come to our aid! And yet how the people of Paris deserve to be saved! . . .

Who can see, unmoved, in the evening, in the streets, the endless queue of housewives at the doors of the canteens, waiting there for a ration of rice or thin soup? At the municipal butcher's, they only distribute once a week, 30 grammes of horsemeat or salt beef. The other days, it is cod or rice. Well! all these faces keep an air of serenity and hope. One feels that one is doing one's duty; but one is sustained by the idea that the provinces are coming to our aid . . . Will they come?‡

Théophile Gautier to Carlotta Grisi:

9th letter, 15 December 1870

What a sad thing it is to be, so to speak, buried alive, and to receive no news of those you love! It is the most grievous part of the torture which we endure, but it will not wear out our constancy . . . Nearly all the last balloons have fallen into the enemy lines. Fog, rain and snow, the time of migration which has come, disturb the flight of our aerial messengers. Alas! I have missed your birthday, I shall miss Christmas and New Year's Day, for I am much afraid that 1871 will find us still besieged. I dare not say anything to you in a letter which may be intercepted like the rest, but do believe that through these fearful catastrophes, which are perhaps unexampled in the history of the world, my thoughts very often fly to you.*

Felix Whitehurst:

15 December

We are not talking so much about fighting as we were, but then death is very busy among us. Not only does it seem that the Prussian shells are venomous, but that the air – or want of it – in the hospitals, joined too to most unhealthy weather, is very fatal [*sic*].†

It is impossible to give precise data respecting the store of provisions now in Paris [continued Labouchère, the same day], nor even were I able would it be fair to do so. As a matter of private opinion, however, I do not think that it will be possible to prolong the resistance beyond the first week in January at the latest. Last Sunday there were incipient bread-riots. By one o'clock all the bakers had closed their shops in the outer faubourg. There had been a run upon them, because a decree had been issued in the morning forbidding flour to be sold, and requisitioning all the biscuits in stock. Government immediately placarded a declaration that bread was not going to be requisitioned, and the explanation of the morning's decree is that flour and not corn has run short, but that new steam-mills are being erected to meet the difficulty. *La Vérité*, a newspaper usually well informed, says that for some days past the flour which had been stored in the town by M. Clément Duvernois has been exhausted, and that we are now living on the corn and meal which was introduced at the last moment from the neighbouring departments. It gives the following calculation of our resources – flour three weeks, corn three months, salt meat fifteen days, horse two months. The mistake of all these calculations seems to be that they do not take into account the fact that more bread or more corn will be eaten when they become the sole means of providing for the population. Thus the daily amount of flour sold in Paris is about one-third above the average. The reason is simple, and yet it seems to occur to no one. French people, particularly the poorer classes, can exist upon much less than Englishmen; but the prospect for any one blessed with a good appetite is by no means reassuring. In the Rue Blanche there is a butcher who sells dogs, cats, and rats. He has many customers, but it is amusing to see them sneak into the shop after carefully looking round to make sure that none of their acquaintances are near ... I own that I have a guilty feeling when I eat dog, the friend of man. I had a slice of a spaniel the other day, and it was by no means bad, something like lamb, but I felt like a cannibal. Epicures in dog flesh tell me that poodle is by far the best, and recommend me to avoid bull dog, which is coarse and tasteless. I really think that dogs have some means of communicating with each other, and have discovered that their old friends want to devour them. The humblest of street curs growls when anyone looks at him.*

It was clear that Paris could not hold out for much longer. On 20 December, from Bordeaux, Lord Lyons, the British Ambassador to France, wrote to Mr Layard, the British Minister at Madrid:

The French want either a peace without cession of territory; or an armistice with the revictualling of Paris for the number of days it lasts; or a European Congress to settle the terms of peace between France and Germany. Bismarck peremptorily rejects all three proposals, and does not say precisely what his conditions of peace are. I suppose the King of Prussia holds to taking Paris as a satisfaction to military vanity, and that if the military situation continues favourable to Germany, he will accept nothing much short of unconditional surrender, while Paris resist. Of course, unless by a miracle, Paris is relieved, its surrender is a question of time – but of how much time ?†

Felix Whitehurst:

25 December

A merry Christmas! I had to break the ice in my bath, and thaw my toothbrush and sponge by the fire . . .

A merry Christmas! When there is nothing to make merry with, and nobody with whom to make merry. Hospitals crowded with the dying; heaps of dead on our surrounding heights; hardly a family which is not in mourning, and even in grief, which is quite another thing; starvation staring us in the face; fuel burnt out; meat a recollection, and vegetables a pleasing dream. Oh yes! by all manner of means a merry Christmas.*

Christmas is not here the great holiday of the year, as it is in England [reported Labouchère on Christmas Day]. Still, everyone in ordinary times tries to have a better dinner than usual, and usually where there are children in a family some attempt is made to amuse them. Among the bourgeoisie they are told to put their shoes in the grate on Christmas-eve, and the next morning some present is found in them, which is supposed to have been left during the night by the Infant Jesus. Since the Empire introduced English ways here, plum-pudding and mince-pies have been eaten, and even Christmas-trees have flourished. This year these festive shrubs, as an invention of the detested foe, have been rigidly tabooed. Plum-puddings and mince-pies, too, will appear on few tables. In order to comfort the children, the girls are to be given soup-tickets to distribute to beggars, and the boys are to have their choice between French and German wooden soldiers. The former will be treasured up, the latter will be subjected to fearful tortures. Even the midnight mass, which is usually celebrated on Christmas-eve, took place in very few churches last night. We have, indeed, too much on our hands to attend either to fasts or festivals, although in the opinion of the *Univers*, the last sortie would have been far more successful had it taken place on the 7th of the month, the anniversary of the promulgation of the Immaculate Conception. Among fine people New Year's-day is more of a fête than Christmas.

Its approach is regarded with dark misgivings by many, for every
gentleman is expected to make a call upon all the ladies of his acquaintance, and to leave them a box of sugarplums. This is a heavy tax upon
those who have more friends than money – 300 fr. is not considered
an extraordinary sum to spend upon these bonbonnières. A friend
of mine, indeed, assured me that he yearly spent 1000 fr., but then
he was a notorious liar, so very possibly he was not telling the truth.
'Thank Heaven,' say the men, 'at least we shall get off the sugarplum
tax this year.' But the ladies are not to be done out of their rights this
way, and they throw out very strong hints that if sugarplums are out
of season, anything solid is very much in season. A dandy who is
known to have a stock of sausages, is overwhelmed with compliments
by his fair friends. A good leg of mutton would, I am sure, win the
heart of the proudest beauty, and by the gift of half-a-dozen potatoes
you might make a friend for life. The English here are making feeble
attempts to celebrate Christmas correctly. In an English restaurant
two turkeys had been treasured up for the important occasion, but
unfortunately a few days ago they anticipated their fate, and most ill-
naturedly insisted upon dying. One fortunate Briton has got ten
pounds of camel, and has invited about twenty of his countrymen
to aid him in devouring this singular substitute for turkey.*

Théophile Gautier:

It is eight o'clock in the evening. Our sober siege dinner is already
absorbed and digested. But we cannot go to bed yet, for the December
dawn rises late. Let us go and visit a friend of our own age; the young
are on the ramparts or on the plain of Avron. Happy the young! They
are not obliged by weakness to remain seated at the gate of Scaea,
like the old man in Homer, while the Greeks and Trojans fight on the
plain. We go out. The night is a sinister black, lashed by a driving
wind and rain mingled with flakes of half-melted snow. The steam
pumps set up on the quai give out a livid smoke through the darkness.
The Seine rolls its waters, ink-coloured, thick, oily as those of the
Styx or the Acheron. At brief intervals, with a lantern on the prow,

a lantern on the poop, projecting a glimmer from their cabin windows, the bateaux-mouches pass by. They stop at the landing-places and, by lamplight, through a vague swarm of shadows, one makes out curious groups of fantastic and spectral appearance. These are the wounded who are being brought back; at least they will not stay on the battlefield until the pale winter morning, and the cold of night will not weld them with their coagulated blood to the glacial and hardened mud. Carriages and stretchers take them to the field hospital where the most assiduous care awaits them. Their glorious day is done, and if their pain allows them to sleep, they will dream of victory and liberation.

On the unlit façade of the Louvre, on the other side of the water, two big windows are ablaze with bursts of reddish light which would make you think it was on fire inside. Against this luminous background, like magic lantern figures badly applied to the slide, vague silhouettes come and go, occupied in some mysterious task. The anhelation of a bellows effaces or clarifies them, by making the light more or less bright. But behind this square, as one might easily have imagined in Romantic times, there is no Ruggieri preparing poisons, no alchemist seeking the philosopher's stone in the depths of his retorts. What produces this disturbing light is quite simply a forge where they are repairing the rifles of the militia and the National Guards.

We cross the pont des Saints-Pères, roughly handled by the antics of the cold wind which tried to blow our hat into the river, an excellent farce *à la Gavroche* which would have seemed in bad taste at that moment. In the distance, as in the shadowy etchings of Piranese, one could make out masses of dim buildings and lines of quais traced by brilliant points like those pinpricks in black cardboard which you hold up to the light; but the pearls of fire were very loosely strung out, and they no longer formed a sparkling chain, the usual illumination of Paris.

The impression was sad, solemn and grand. Through the wide openings guarded by the colossal statues of Peace and War, the place du Carrousel appeared glistening with water, glazed with reflections, and crossed by a single omnibus whose red lanterns gleamed like the eyes of a monstrous insect crawling in the gloom.

We followed several streets, which were so dark that they looked like saw-marks in blocks of black marble; finally we reached our friend's house. He had gone *for news*, for that is still the food one seeks most avidly, however poor the fare that we eat. And so we were obliged to return to our lodging, and there, feet up against a little widow's fire, with a *single* candle for light (in time of siege one has to save both fire and heat), we took a book at random from the pine-wood plank which carries the wreckage of our library, and sadly began our evening of solitude.*

A French naval officer:

25 December

The cold is growing intense . . . The suffering of the troops is excessive; there are cases of frostbite in the trenches. The Government announces that all the troops which are not needed to guard occupied positions are to come back into Paris. This move does not in any way, so it is said, imply the relinquishing of operations which have been begun; the defence will be continued, at whatever sacrifice, until final victory.

This language is in perfect accord with public opinion; unfortunately it does not agree with the spirit that reigns in the army. Whole regiments are crying: 'Long live peace!' and this is the cry which greeted the Governor himself on a recent visit to one of our works.

Fortunately the demoralisation of the enemy troops appears no less great. At Ville-Évrard, some Saxons gave themselves up of their own accord, as prisoners, to a second-lieutenant of the 103rd.†

Field-Marshal Count von Blumenthal:

26 December

It is abominably cold, and now Mont Valérien has begun again, right lustily, so as to make my windows rattle . . .

I am more and more convinced that my plan for reducing Paris, viz.,
by starvation, is the right one.

The argument that this will take too long I cannot allow.*

Henri Dabot:

At my friend J—'s I ate a big house-sparrow, garnished with mush-
rooms. His son had caught it in a bird-trap, treacherously set on his
balcony. He had lain in wait for it for a long time on my account,
to thank me for some sweets I had given him.†

Felix Whitehurst:

Castor and Pollux died yesterday in their 7th year. They are being
sold today on the Boulevard Haussmann. When alive they were
elephants; now dead, they are beef.

It was much too cold to see the old year out, so, as residents in
Paris, we drank, in the very coldest of weather, confusion to the last
hours of that fatal year 1870, and went to bed to the pleasing melody
of minute guns from all the forts, which music lasted all night, and
awoke us up to the new life of 1871.‡

V *JANUARY 1871*

Mme Edgar Quinet:

1 January 1871

Everyone is thinking today of the most useful New Year presents. Instead of those bunches of artificial flowers, mounted on brass wire, the traditional sweets and chocolate drops, those who are privileged by fortune give you a wing of chicken or a piece of cheese in an elegant paper cornet. I myself was given a little jewel in bronze, very pretty, made from a shell splinter. It represented the carrier pigeon of the Republic.*

The Crown Prince of Prussia to Queen Victoria:

Headquarters, Versailles,
3 January 1871

It would surely be no shame to France that has fought bravely, to confess at last that she has been beaten by an Army equal to hers . . .

That we Germans are losing hold of sympathy in England I have already observed for a long time with grief, and this will go on increasingly till Paris falls, especially as the bombardment of the forts is now to begin . . .†

Henri Dabot:

5 January

Recommended procedure for making a shell harmless
Plunge the projectile into water so that it stands on its bottom; wait for an hour to allow the water to penetrate into the shell and drench the powder.

Hardly had I stuck this procedure into my notebook, when there was a formidable bang. I rushed into the street and ran towards the Luxembourg, where everyone was running. A shell had fallen at the corner of the old rue Sainte-Catherine d'Enfer; another had staved in the roof of the Dames Saint-Michel; a third the roof of the institution

Barbet; a fourth had entered the apartments at No. 36, rue Gay-
Lussac. The splinters of the first shell were picked up with feverish
enthusiasm. They smelt of powder and pitch...

I went home again to close the shutters.*

Felix Whitehurst:

6 January

Shells fell in the city of Paris near the Panthéon, the Luxembourg,
and in the market at Montrouge; but no lives are reported lost. The
unjustifiable proceeding of bombarding a beleaguered city after some
110 days' investment, seems to have astonished, and rather shocked,
our simple-minded rulers ...†

BOMBARDMENT OF PARIS
PROTEST BY THE GOVERNMENT OF
NATIONAL DEFENCE

We denounce to the Cabinets of Europe, to world opinion, the treat-
ment which the Prussian Army does not fear to inflict on the city of
Paris ...

It will soon be four months since the army laid siege to this great
capital, and held its 2,400,000 inhabitants as captives.

It had flattered itself that it would reduce them in a few days. It
counted on sedition and on weakness.

Since these auxiliaries were lacking, it called famine to its aid.

Having surprised the besieged capital deprived of a relieving army
and even of organized Gardes nationaux, the army surrounded it at
its ease with formidable works, bristling with batteries, which hurl
death for eight kilometres.

Withdrawn behind this rampart, the Prussian army repelled the
offensives of the garrison.

Then it began to bombard some of the forts.

Paris remained firm.

Then, without preliminary warning, the Prussian army directed enormous projectiles against the city; its formidable guns allow it to overwhelm the city from two leagues away.

This violence has continued for the past four days.

Last night, more than two thousand shells overwhelmed the quartiers of Montrouge, Grenelle, Auteuil, Passy, Saint-Jacques and Saint-Germain.

It seems that they were directed wantonly on the hospitals, the ambulances, the prisons, churches and schools.

The Government of National Defence strongly protests to the civilized world at this act of useless brutality, and warmly associates itself with the feelings of the indignant population who, far from letting themselves be cowed by this violence, find in it new strength to fight and to repel the shame of the foreign invaders.*

Albert Vandam:

I know nothing of the military import of a bombardment, but have been told that even the greatest strategists only count upon the moral effect it produces upon the besieged inhabitants. I can only say this: if Marshal von Moltke took the 'moral effect' of his projectiles into his calculations to accelerate the surrender of Paris, he might have gone on shelling Paris for a twelvemonth without being one whit nearer his aim; that is, if I am to judge by the scene I witnessed on that January morning . . . At the risk of offending all the sensation-mongers, foreign and native, with pen or with pencil, I can honestly say that a broken-down omnibus and a couple of prostrate horses would have excited as much curiosity as did the sight of the battered tenements at Vaugirard, Montrouge, and Vanves. On the Chaussée du Maine, the roadway had been ploughed up, for a distance of about half a dozen yards, by a shell; in another spot, a shell had gone clean through the roof and killed a woman by the side of her husband; in a third, a shell had carried away part of the wall of a one-storied cottage, and the whole of the opposite wall: in short, there was more than sufficient evidence that life was no longer safe within the fortifications, and yet there was no wailing, no wringing of hands, no heartrending frenzied look of despair, either pent up or endeavouring to find vent in shrieks and yells, nay, not even on the part of the women. There was merely a kind of undemonstrative contempt – very unlike the usual French way of manifesting it – blended with a considerable dash of *badauderie*, – for which word I cannot find an English equivalent, because the Parisian loafer or idler is unlike any of his European congeners... The nearest approach to him is the middle-class English tourist on the Continent, who endeavours to explain to his wife and companions things he does not know himself, and blesses his stars aloud for having made him an Englishman.

But even the Paris badaud, who is not unlike his Roman predecessor in his craving for circuses, must have bread; and when the cry arises, a fortnight later, that 'there is no more bread', the siege is virtually at an end.*

Major William Blumé, Prussian Ministry of War:

Mid January

The whole number of guns brought into action against the south front of Paris, by the middle of January, was 123; forty being in first line. The whole of the city on the left bank of the Seine, and the following quarters on the right bank, were within range, viz., Passy, Auteuil, Boulogne, and Billancourt; two hundred or three hundred shells were thrown into them every day, which, without doing any serious damage, were yet enough to scare away most of the inhabitants, shake their nerves and energy, and weaken their determination to resist . . .

It became daily more evident that the capabilities of Paris for resistance were nearly at an end. Even if there had been a more ample supply of provisions, the endurance of the defenders must have given way soon; for from the north, too, the heavy siege-guns were closing on them with their far-ranging and accurate fire, and the moment was not perhaps far distant when the northern quarters of Paris would be exposed to the terrors of a bombardment.†

Richard Wallace to Jules Favre, Minister for Foreign Affairs:

Paris, 14 January

Monsieur le Ministre,

The wonderful behaviour of the Parisians in those neighbourhoods so brutally bombarded has given me an idea which I should like to offer you: an idea which, I hope, will be warmly welcomed and appreciated by the inhabitants of the capital.

I should like a patriotic subscription to be opened in Paris immediately: a subscription in aid of the unfortunate families which have been obliged to flee their lodgings under enemy fire, so as to distribute to them at once the help of every kind of which they have so urgent a need.

Should my proposal receive the approval of the Government of National Defence, I should be glad if you would put my name down on this list for the sum of one hundred thousand francs, which I shall pay in at once to the treasury, so that the distribution of the aid I mention may begin forthwith.

I have the honour to be, with deep respect, Monsieur le Ministre, Your Excellency's most humble and most obedient servant,

RICHARD WALLACE*

Jules Favre, Minister for Foreign Affairs, to Richard Wallace:

Paris, 15 January 1871

Sir,

I accept your generous offer with appreciation, and I beg you, in the name of the Government, in the name of the city of Paris whose interpreter I am, to receive the expression of our feelings of gratitude. You have already contributed powerfully to relieve the sufferings which heaven imposes on us. Your presence among us, your abundant liberalities will make your name blessed by the people of Paris. The awareness of the great duty which it accomplishes makes it remain calm in the presence of the enemy's violence; it will draw new strength from the certainty of effective help in which all men of feeling will share, and they thank you, Sir, for having taken this initiative.

I beg you, Sir, to accept the assurance of the feelings of high esteem with which I have the honour to be

Your most humble and most obedient servant,

JULES FAVRE*

The bombardment still continues [Labouchère reported that day]. The cannon now make one continuous noise. Each particular discharge cannot be distinguished. The shells fall on the left bank to a distance of about a mile from the ramparts. A return of the *Official Journal* gives 138 wounded and fifty-one killed up to the 13th. Among the killed are eighteen children and twelve women; among the wounded, twenty-one children and forty-five women. Waggons and hand-carts packed with household goods are streaming in from the left to the right bank. In the bombarded quarters many shops are closed. Some householders have made a sort of casemate reaching to the first story of their houses; others sleep in their cellars. The streets are, however, full of people, even in the most exposed districts; and all the heights from which a view is to be had of the Prussian batteries are crowded with sightseers. Every now and then one comes across some house through which a shell has passed. The public buildings have, as yet, suffered very slightly. The dome of the Panthéon, which we presume is used as a mark for the aim of the Prussian artillerymen, has been hit once. The shell had made a round hole in the dome, and it burst inside the church. In the Jardin des Plantes all the glass of the conservatories has been shattered by the concussion of the air, and the orchids and other tropical plants are dying. Although war and its horrors are thus brought home to our very doors, it is even still difficult to realise that great events are passing around us which history will celebrate in its most solemn and dignified style. Distance in battles lends grandeur to the view. Had the charge of Balaclava taken place on Clapham Common, or had our gallant swordsmen replaced the donkeys on Hampstead Heath, even Tennyson would have been unable to poetise their exploits. When one sees stuck up in an omnibus-office that omnibuses 'will have to make a circuit from

Preparing for the defence of Paris

cause de bombardement'; when shells burst in restaurants and maim the waiters; when the trenches are in tea-gardens; and when one is invited for a sou to look through a telescope at the enemy firing off their guns, there is a homely domestic air about the whole thing which is quite inconsistent with 'the pomp and pride of glorious war . . .'

We hear now that Government is undertaking an inquiry to discover precisely how long our stock of provisions will last. Matters are managed so carelessly, that I doubt whether the Minister of Commerce himself knows to within ten days the precise date when we shall be starved out. The rations of meat now amount to 1–27th of a pound per diem for each adult. At the fashionable restaurants the supply is unlimited, and the price as unlimited. Two cutlets of donkey cost 18 francs, and everything else in the way of animal food is in proportion. The real vital question, however, is how long the bread will last. In some arrondissements the supply fails after 8 o'clock in the morning; at others, each resident receives 1 lb upon production of a *carte de subsistance*. The distribution has been thrown into disorder by the people from the bombarded quarters flocking into the central ones, and wanting to be fed . . . Jules and Jacques will hereafter quaff many a petit verre to their own heroism; and many a story will they inflict upon their long-suffering friends redounding to their own special glory. Their wives will be told that they ought to be proud to have such men for husbands. But Jules and Jacques are in reality but arrant humbugs. Whilst they boozed, their wives starved; whilst they were warmly clad, their wives were in rags; whilst they were drinking confusion to their enemies in some snug room, their wives were freezing at the baker's door for their ration of bread. In Paris the women – I speak of those of the poorer classes – are of more sterling stuff than the men. They suffer far more, and they repine much less. I admire the crowd of silent, patient women, huddling together for warmth every morning, as they wait until their pittance is doled out to them, far more than the martial heroes who foot it behind a drum and a trumpet to crown a statue, to visit a tomb, and to take their turn on the ramparts; or the heroes of the pen, who day after day, from some cosy office, issue a manifesto announcing that victory is certain, because they have made a pact with death.*

Felix Whitehurst:

16 January

120th day of the siege . . . Every minute the dead silence of Paris night, as it is now without conveyances, was broken by one or two explosions which shook your very tooth-brush in its frozen glass. The 'Official Journal' is ominously silent as to what the effect . . . of 36 hours of heavy bombarding has been.†

On 18 January, King William of Prussia was proclaimed Emperor of the newly-constituted German Empire. The ceremony was held in the Hall of Mirrors at Versailles.

Two days later Clémentine of Coburg wrote to Queen Victoria. She was the daughter of Louis-Philippe, and she was married to the Queen's first cousin, Prince Augustus.

Dear Victoria,

How can *you*, the happy Queen of a great and splendid Empire, *you*, whose generous soul, whose good and compassionate heart I understand: how can *you* not raise your voice to save the lives of thousands of women and children, and to prevent the bombardment, the destruction of Paris, of that beautiful Paris which welcomed you so warmly, and acclaimed you with enthusiasm? How can free, rich and mighty England do nothing to put an end to the ambition and barbarity of the new Emperor of Germany, and help my heroic compatriots to save France? . . .

Cousin, you will forgive me, your old friend, for having spoken to you so frankly, and you will let me sign myself always, my dear Victoria, your most devoted Cousin and friend,

CLÉMENTINE‡

Field-Marshal Count Helmuth von Moltke:

There was absolutely no expedient possible but the capitulation of the capital; every delay intensified the necessity, and enforced the acceptance of harder terms. Unless all the railways were at once thrown open for the transport of supplies from a very wide area, the horrors of famine would inevitably fall on a population of more than two million souls; and later it might not be practicable to cope with the emergency. Yet no one dared utter the fatal word 'capitulation', no one would undertake the responsibility for the inevitable.

A great council of war was held on the 21st. In it all the elder Generals pronounced any further measures to be quite impossible. It was proposed that a council of the younger officers should also be held, but no decision was arrived at. As, however, someone must be made answerable for every misfortune, General Trochu, originally the most popular member of the Government, was dismissed from his post as Governor, and the chief military command was entrusted to General Vinoy. General Ducrot resigned his command.

All this did nothing to improve the situation, so on the 23rd, Monsieur Jules Favre made his appearance at Versailles to negotiate in the first instance for an armistice.

On the German side there was readiness to meet this request; but, of course, some guarantee had to be forthcoming that the capital, after having been reprovisioned, would not renew its resistance. The surrender of the forts, inclusive of Mont Valérien and the town of St Denis, as well as the disarmament of the enceinte was demanded and acceded to.*

Madame Edgar Quinet:

24 January, in the evening
The horrible eventuality of the capitulation of Paris presents itself to our minds for the first time.†

Edwin Child, of the Garde civique:

25 January
Up at 9. Appel at 11, gave my resignation to the Captain, feeling heartily disgusted with the whole affair. 400,000 men capitulating, granted half of them of no use as soldiers, *soit* 200,000. I pity the people, but scorn the chiefs, after the entire confidence placed in them

by the people something might have been done, had half the population been sacrificed to the enemy there would have been no recriminations but after passing a winter pareil & all for nothing, the population seem as if paralysed and unable to comprehend their position, and the Government are afraid to say the word 'capitulation', so call it 'armistice' what an end of 20 years of uninterrupted prosperity, & what a lesson to a nation fond of flattery and calling itself the vanguard of civilization . . .

Provisions have fallen as if by enchantment & yet none have entered the city, a convincing proof that a few scoundrels have been speculating upon the general misery.*

Field-Marshal Count Helmuth von Moltke:

Hostilities were to be suspended on the evening of the 26th, so far as Paris was concerned, and all supplies to be freely given. A general armistice of twenty-one days was then to come into force on the 31st of January, exclusive, however, of the departments of Doubs, Jura, and Côte d'or, and the fortress of Belfort, where for the time operations were still being carried on, in which both sides were hopeful of success.

This armistice gave the Government of National Defence the time necessary for assembling a freely elected National Assembly at Bordeaux, which should decide whether the war should be continued, or on what conditions peace should be concluded.†

Lieutenant-Colonel du Génie Brunon: Commanding Officer of the Fort of Vanves:

27 January

Like all the army commanders and heads of important services, we were called to the Ministry of War at eight o'clock, to be given some important information.

When we had all assembled in one of the rooms at the Ministry of War, the Governor, General Trochu, spoke to us [*sic*], and set out clearly, almost in these terms, the situation of Paris. He said that it

only had enough food for another two or three days, and in order not
to let so large and brave a population die of famine, the Government
had found itself in the painful necessity of entering into negotiations
with the enemy.

He then announced the conditions of the convention which had
been drawn up. They seemed excessive to a garrison – and to an army
– which had always done their duty, and which had asked repeatedly
to march against the enemy.

He finally added, with tears in his eyes, and this was his greatest
regret, that the members of the Government of National Defence had
never been prepared to let him go to Versailles himself and fight for,
and maintain, the army's interests . . .

We dispersed with deep sadness at heart: the defence of Paris and
of France was over!*

Part Three

The Troubled
Peace

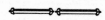

JANUARY–MARCH 1871

Henri Dabot:

28 January

At two o'clock in the morning I mount guard in the place du Panthéon. A terrifying silence follows the sinister sound of the shells,
the infernal din of the forts, which are henceforth dumb. The dome
of the Panthéon rises proudly, despite its wounds. The wan light of
the oil lamps gives one a glimpse of the broken capital on one of the
pillars of the École de Droit. 'Keep your eyes open,' they say to me,
'groups of rioters may come into the place du Panthéon. If you see
them, come back and shout: "To arms!"'

The plans for capitulation have in fact been greeted with suppressed
fury.

Friends, who were sent out for news, come back and tell us that the
mob is being roused at Belleville. But what can one do? We hardly
have any more bread – and what bread! I am obliged to stride energetically up and down the pavements of the rue Soufflot to get down
the chaff of oats which I've swallowed under the name of bread.

As I come off guard, I feel almost ill, I am so moved to have seen
at close quarters the sufferings of the poor. They are queueing outside
the mairie to have coupons for soup.*

Un Bourgeois de Paris:

This morning everyone rushed for the *Officiel*. This is what it said:

PROCLAMATION BY THE GOVERNMENT
TO THE CITIZENS OF PARIS

Citizens,

The convention which ends the resistance of Paris is not yet signed,
but there is only a few hours' delay.

The basis remains fixed as we announced yesterday.

The enemy will not come inside the fortifications of Paris.

The National Guard will keep its organization and its weapons.

A division of twelve thousand men remains intact; as for the other troops, they will stay in Paris, in our midst, instead of being cantoned in the suburbs, as had been originally proposed. The officers will keep their swords.

We shall publish the articles of the convention as soon as the signatures have been exchanged, and at the same time we shall publish the exact state of our provisions.

Paris wants to be sure that the resistance lasted to the absolute limits of possibility. The figures we give will be irrefutable proof, and we shall challenge anyone to contest them.

We shall show that there remains only just enough bread to last until revictualling, and that we could not have prolonged the struggle without condemning two million men, women and children to certain death.

The siege of Paris lasted for four months and twelve days; the bombardment lasted a whole month. Since 15 January the bread ration has been reduced to 300 grammes; since 15 December, the horsemeat ration has been only 30 grammes. Mortality has more than trebled. Amidst all these disasters, there has not been a single day of discouragement.

The enemy is the first to pay tribute to the moral energy and courage which the whole population of Paris has just displayed. Paris has suffered greatly; but the Republic will profit from its long sufferings, so nobly borne. We come out of the struggle which has ended, strengthened for the struggle to come. We come out of it with all our honour, and with all our hopes, despite the sorrows of the present hour; more than ever we have faith in the destiny of our native country.*

The Crown Prince of Germany to Queen Victoria:

Telegram
Versailles, 29 January 1871

Three weeks' Armistice. Today we occupy all the forts round Paris, garrison prisoners of war.†

Field-Marshal Count Helmuth von Moltke:

The forts were occupied on the 29th without opposition.

There were taken over from the Field Army of Paris 602 guns, 1,770,000 stand of arms, and above 1000 ammunition waggons; from the fortress 1362 heavy guns, 1680 gun-carriages, 860 limbers, 3,500,000 cartridges, 4000 hundred-weight of powder, 200,000 shells, and 100,000 bombs.

The blockade of Paris, which had lasted 132 days, was over, and the greater part of the German forces which had so long stood fast under its walls, was released to end the war in the open field.*

Mme Edgar Quinet:

It was with horror and stupor that Paris read the clauses of the armistice this morning, the text of the Convention signed by M. de Bismarck and the Minister for Foreign Affairs. The final insult, added to the cruelty, was to describe as an armistice this surrender to the mercy of the Prussians. The army a prisoner of war! All our cannon handed over! An indemnity of two hundred millions from Paris!

The national resistance is over the moment that the forts of Paris are in the hands of the enemy.†

Felix Whitehurst:

All is over in Paris, for although it is really only an armistice in order to allow the French to summon a National Assembly, . . . yet it is practically a peace which will be treated for, and must be accepted by France . . .

The Government had to give in at last, a very unpopular measure. But I think that truly great men would have run the gauntlet of the 'Inevitable', and come to terms months ago.

Collectively the Parisians were bold, and all for holding out. Talk to them individually, and they all allowed a month ago: 'Why, of course we can have no chance in the end.'‡

A naval officer:

I have just spent several hours watching the long procession of troops returning in disorder into Paris. For a few eyes that were wet with tears, how many indifferent or even happy faces! How very few, among us, have a sense of the great misfortune which afflicts us! Is it the beginning of irreparable decadence? If, alas, men have failed us, hasn't the country also failed itself?

Will France find her soul again?*

General Ducrot to his wife:

Dear darling, it is all over! My heart is broken with grief and full of fury . . .

Many unjust accusations are being made against those who have directed the defence. It could not be otherwise, with so disastrous a result. No doubt there has been more than one mistake, especially in these latter days; but history will prove that the intentions were pure, and, one day, it will also relate that there was much heroism and much greatness in this resistance to the bitter end.†

Soon after the capitulation, an English observer, Archibald Forbes, paid a visit to the stricken city.

I had intended to promenade Paris all night, to make the most of the time necessarily limited. But before ten o'clock the promenade had become almost a solitary one. By nine the dim lights were put out in the kiosks, and the petroleum was waning in the street lamps. By half-past the cafés were putting up their shutters . . . By ten the world of Paris was left to darkness and to me, and so I went to bed. The midnight air was not tortured by the sound of revellers, although there were no police to keep order. I woke up between twelve and one in the night, and the silence made me for the moment think myself back at Margency.

The whole city was haunted by the peculiar, half-sweetish, half-foetid odour which horseflesh gives out in cooking: an odour which

I had learned to appreciate at Metz. It permeated the deserted British Embassy, where, asserting my privileges as a Briton, I stabled my horse; it lingered in the corridors of the Grand Hotel, and fought with the taint from wounds in evil case. The Grand Hotel was one huge hospital. Half Paris seemed converted into hospitals, if one might judge by the flags. There had been more than were needed until the Southern bombardment began; and then the hospitals, ambulances, orphanages, and madhouses on the Southern side had to be evacuated, there had been quite a squeeze on this side of the water. Very touching was the ignorance everywhere as to the outside world. 'I have seen three English papers since September,' said Dr Gordon, our Medical Commissioner. 'Is Ireland quiet? Is Mr Gladstone still Prime Minister? Is the Princess Louise married? Such were samples of the questions I had to answer.*

Another English visitor was Captain H. M. Hozier, author of *The Franco-Prussian War*:

The aspect of the Bois de Boulogne, the Champs-Élysées, and the boulevards, was [he remembered] most extraordinary ... There were no carriages in the Bois, for most of the owners had fled the city and most of the horses were eaten . . . Thirty to forty thousand horses were eaten. The reader may imagine the void that their absence created . . . There were no carriages at the door of the Jockey Club, no crowd of *voitures* at the Grand Hotel; all were reduced to the democratic omnibus, or the still more democratic Shanks' mare...

Paris the brilliant was not only dirty, but dull. All the theatres were closed by order of the prefect of police at the commencement of the siege; and the scenery and properties packed away in secure places against the danger of fire. The *cafés chantants, casinos*, and all other places of amusement, were also closed, and, with the exception of performances in aid of the funds for the ambulances and other charitable purposes, there were scarcely any means of relaxation in the city for the 80,000 provincial mobiles far away from family and home, and the thousands of national guards; and the poor fellows had no resource but drinking at the wine shops and cafés, or going to bed with the fowls. The streets were miserably dull; in place of two or three gaslights they were lighted with one small petroleum lamp, that looked more like a taper burning before a statue of the Virgin than a street light; and in the bitter, cold, dark nights of January few who had a home of their own troubled the pavements of Paris with their presence.*

Edward Blount to his wife:

31 January

We hope for provisions at the end of the week, but the railways are in an awful state. There is no way of getting to Boulogne or Calais. I am overloaded with work. Her Majesty has named me her Consul, and the Ministers have written me flattering letters. I had to break open the office at the Embassy to get the papers to give passports. Thank Heaven the bombardment is over, and all this carnage. I bought some beef today at six francs a pound. I bought horseflesh, which I distributed among my own clerks and others to save them from starvation.†

Captain Hozier:

The moment the gates were opened the people were seized with uncontrollable yearning for fresh food. The first who brought loaves of white bread, joints of fresh mutton, and vegetables into Paris, were regarded with as much curiosity as artists who had produced new forms of beauty, or searchers who had discovered hidden treasures. To obtain something different from siege fare seemed the sole object of the whole world.‡

Edward Blount:

As soon as the armistice was proclaimed, the London Relief Committee, which had been nobly working all through the siege, and was only waiting its opportunity, despatched its first consignment of food and fuel to Paris by way of Folkestone and Dieppe, as a gift. In the early days of February nearly 10,000 tons of flour, 450 tons of rice,

900 tons of biscuits, 360 tons of fish, and nearly 4000 tons of fuel, with about 7,000 head of live stock, were brought to the relief of Paris . . .

The goods were received with thanks, but when a certain quantity of pheasants and other luxuries were seen by the Delegates of the Provisional Government, they exclaimed: '*Ces choses-là sont pour l'aristocratie et non pour le peuple. Il ne serait pas prudent de les distribuer,*' and, if I remember right, the pheasants and luxuries were sent back to England.*

Ernest A. Vizetelly:

One of the first interesting sights which I witnessed on returning to Paris with my father and my brother Arthur, at the close of the German siege, was the distribution of the provisions which were sent from England, a highly successful Lord Mayor's Fund having been established in London in order to relieve the necessities of the famished Parisians. In the central part of the city the distributions took place at the agency of Messrs Copestake, Moore & Co., on the Place des Victoires, where the queues of emaciated, anxious, waiting people were interminable. In this district everything was conducted in a methodical and highly satisfactory manner; but more than once I heard of grumbling in other parts of Paris where the distributions were left to the local municipal authorities, it being asserted there that some folk were unduly favoured, and that others, who were really in more necessitous circumstances, received very inadequate shares of the British gifts.†

Wickham Hoffman:

The first train of provisions to enter Paris was sent by the citizens of London, to their credit be it spoken. Will it be believed that considerable difficulty was experienced in finding persons willing to take the trouble to distribute food gratuitously? It was done to a very limited extent at the *mairies*. The great dry-food establishment of the Bon Marché distributed a portion; but much was stored in the Halles de l'Abondance for want of distribution, and burned up when that establishment was destroyed during the Commune.*

Ernest A. Vizetelly:

The Grenier d'Abondance, or Reserve Granary, on the Boulevard Bourdon, was a huge establishment, which contained large stores of grain, oil, wine, spirits and dry cod, and which was set on fire by a certain Ulric, commander of the 13th Legion of the National Guard. The conflagration lasted two full days, and a terrible stench (due to the burning oil and codfish) infected the whole neighbourhood.†

Alphonse Daudet:

6 February

And to think that for some people these five months of exhausting sadness have been intoxicating, a perpetual festival! From the idlers in the suburbs who earn their forty-five sous a day for doing nothing, to the majors with seven stripes, contractors for barricades in rooms, ambulance-men as well fed as Gamache all glowing with good meat gravy, dandified sharpshooters preening themselves in the cafés, and simply calling the waiters with omnibus whistles, commandants of the National Guard lodged with their ladies in requisitioned apartments, all the monopolizers, all the exploiters, the dog-stealers, the cat-chasers, the dealers in horses' hooves, in albumin, in gelatine, the pigeon-raisers, the owners of milch cows, and the citizens who have promissory notes with the bailiff, and those who don't like to pay their rents: for all these people the end of the siege is a desolation – which has nothing patriotic about it. With Paris open, they must return to their place among the rank and file, look life in the face, hand back the stripes and apartments, and go back to their hovels. They find it hard.‡

Henry Labouchère:

7 February

Will the Prussians enter Paris? is the question which I have been asked by every Frenchman to whom I have mentioned that I have been at Versailles. This question overshadows every other; and I am fully convinced that this vain, silly population would rather that King William should double the indemnity which he demands from France than march with his troops down the Rue de Rivoli. The fact that they have been conquered is not so bitter to the Parisians as the idea of that fact being brought home to them by the presence of their con-querors even for half-an-hour within the walls of the sacred city. I have no very great sympathy with the desire of the Prussians to march through Paris; and I have no great sympathy with the horror which is felt by the Parisians at their intention to do so. The Prussian flag waves over the forts, and consequently to all intents and purposes Paris has capitulated. A triumphal march along the main streets will not mend matters, nor mar matters. 'Attila without' stands before vanquished Paris, as the Cimbrian slave did before Marius. The sword drops from his hand; 'awed by the majesty of the past, he flees and dares not strike,' is the way in which a newspaper I have just bought deals with the question. It is precisely this sort of nonsense which makes the Prussians determined that the Parisians shall drink the cup of humiliation to its last dregs.*

Field-Marshal Count von Blumenthal:

11 February

Immediately after the armistice is over Paris will be occupied by us, and this ought to take the pride out of this absurdly vain people.

All the utterances of the people in Versailles and those who come out of Paris show them to be very depressed, but not entirely dis-couraged. We are acting a great deal too leniently towards the country, and we shall surely regret that we have not taken stronger measures with it. The French mistake our leniency for weakness.†

Carlotta Grisi to Théophile Gautier:

Geneva, 16 February 1871

My dear Théophile,

I learn that you are getting letters, so I am resuming mine, and the first thing I ask you is to write to us often, for we still haven't had a

line from you since the armistice, and this has worried us very much;
but I received a letter from my sister this morning, and she told us
that she had seen you, and, if you were exhausted, at least you were
still there. Since you say nothing about your news, I thought that
perhaps you intended to pay a visit to Geneva; but the railways are
not working beyond Paris, and you mustn't risk getting held up on
the way. I really don't know what to think any more.

The children are well, they are working very hard for the prisoners
of war. Those poor soldiers! It was pitiful to see them arrive, some
with frozen feet, others with hardly any clothes, some with women's
skirts to cover themselves, one had never seen anything more heartrending. The poor devils are very happy to be here, where people are
doing all that is humanly possible for them.

And you, too, my poor friends, have suffered much, believe that we
have often thought of you, and I can say that I blessed God the day I
learned of the armistice, for I said to myself that henceforward the
people I love were safe from fresh misfortunes.

I want these few lines to reach you as soon as possible, and so I'll
finish my letter another time. For the moment I embrace you ten-
derly, and I am with all my heart your affectionate

CARLOTTA GRISI*

Théophile Gautier to Carlotta Grisi:

Paris, February 1871

After five months in a dungeon they half open our prison door; they
lift the lid off our coffin and we can at last renew our relations with
the living world. Telegrams are beginning to arrive with one or two
months' delay ... How joyfully I recognised the little blue monogram
announcing a missive from Geneva I need not say: you can well
imagine it. It's no good knowing that reply is impossible, you grow
sad at writing letters which seem to be lost in space and you end up
by believing that people forget you; it isn't the famine or the rain of
shells that has been most painful in Paris, it has been this sequestra-
tion, this horrible isolation that kept you apart from your friendships

and family affections, from all that touched your heart, that left you ignorant of what was happening a mile beyond the city. We were absolutely cut off from the world, not knowing what they did in the provinces, whether or not they were coming to our aid, abandoned by the universe, deprived of all spiritual consolation, reduced to the most fearful extremities. All that was nothing beside this anguish, this waiting which was always disappointed. A pigeon came back with half its feathers gone. Still no letter! One no longer dared to say: It will come next time. On your saint's day, at Christmas, on New Year's Day, at the happy times when I used to go and see you, I felt dull with melancholy, exhausted with grief. I yearned for that Saint-Jean which, alas, you no longer inhabit! that Saint-Jean which framed your beloved image so well in my memory. How I have thirsted since the armistice to leave Paris and see you again, to live a normal life for a little while by your side!

From the day when I bade you farewell on the Montreux boat, my existence has only been a long nightmare, a reversal of reality, a series of catastrophes so wildly impossible that my soul, despite the evidence, still refuses to believe them.*

22 February 1871

My dear Carlotta,

I have been very tired by my illness; the convalescence took longer than it would have taken in any other circumstances. But it is not easy to recover during a siege the last weeks of which recalled the raft of the *Medusa* of famishing memory. An ounce of horse a day and 200 grams of bread which looked like turf-dust are not a diet to restore your strength. We held on beyond the limits of possibility and many people died of hunger under the less alarming title of anaemia. As for myself, I don't know if I should have held out another fortnight. The moment was approaching when we should have had to toss for who should be eaten. We were so concerned about finding some or other broken meat, even a dead rat, that we paid no attention to the shells. We had come down to cutting old hides into strips, soaking them in water and making them into forcemeat balls which passed for a delicacy. Old cabbage leaves were being sold for 10 sous each; we bore it all in the hope that the provinces would come to our aid. Paris can say, like François I: 'All is lost save honour.' However crushed we may be, there is no shame in being French. How grateful I am to you for the kindness which you show our poor soldiers, so wretched, so bereft of everything, so overwhelmed by every hardship . . .*

The siege was over, and the peace terms were about to be settled; and yet, to foreign observers, Paris seemed, even now, to be unaware of reality. Late in February, from Mont Valérien, the great fort which the Prussians now occupied, the subaltern in the Garde Landwehr reported:

The Parisians, and more particularly still, *les Parisiennes*, are behaving in the most wonderfully joyous manner . . . Strange, passing strange it is. Here we have clasped their beautiful city in our grasp – here we are, conquerors at their very gates – and still the Parisians will never, never confess that they are conquered. '*Allons donc, Monsieur*,' I have heard again and again. '*C'est une convention, pas une capitulation!*' It would seem that they still regard it as an absolute impossibility that we should march into their sacred city. I am firmly convinced that, after we have left France, the French will talk themselves into the belief that they have driven us from their land, and that they are the conquerors, not the conquered! . . .

Never before have I realised the matchless beauty of Paris so fully as this morning. Even as I write, the still grey dawn of early morning hovers above the city; but, one by one, the towers become visible. The *Colonne Vendôme* is just emerging, slowly and majestically, from the gloom, and already I can trace the faint outlines of the *July Column*, somewhat further off. All is still and noiseless as yet, and here, at the bastion, you hear as yet only the clocks of the great church steeples as they strike the hours. Well, but a few days hence, I hope, we shall pass through the *Arc de Triomphe* with banners flying and music playing!*

On 1 March the German army was to occupy Paris, and to stay there until the peace terms had been ratified. The Parisians awaited this supreme humiliation with their usual sense of theatre: indeed, even Edmond Got, a *sociétaire* of the Comédie-Française, wondered if the event was to smack too much of the stage. On 27 February he noted in his diary:

This evening, at dead of night, Carpeaux [the sculptor], with a few friends equipped with ladders borrowed from the Ministère de la Marine, veiled with crape the eight stone figures of the cities of France, the statues round the place de la Concorde . . .

It's too theatrical, perhaps . . . But the sight will be terrible, especially if the space they invade, empty of Frenchmen as I hope, leaves the enemy alone under the gaze of these grandiose and menacing witnesses.†

Field-Marshal Count von Blumenthal:

1 March

At nine o'clock we drove to Suresnes. Thence we went on foot, and at the Tribune in Longchamp we mounted our horses, on the very spot where, in 1867, I stood with my Adjutant, Von Bredon, to see the great review of the French troops before the Emperor of Austria.

At that time I was much annoyed (and I said so to Bredon) at the arrogant expression in the faces of the French Marshals and the Generals. I said to him, also, that I hoped we should ourselves soon hold a grand parade here, too. That it would ever come true I had never a suspicion.

Today 30,000 men belonging to the First, Eleventh, and Second Bavarian Army Corps were drawn up here.

The Kaiser arrived, inspected the troops, and then the march towards Paris began.

With the Dukes of Coburg, Gottberg, and others, I placed myself at the head of the column, and we marched through the Bois de Boulogne – terribly devastated – and the Avenue de l'Impératrice to the Arc de l'Étoile, and thence along the Champs-Élysées to the obelisk on the Place de la Concorde.*

Felix Whitehurst:

The troops were to enter Paris at 10 a.m.; but at 8.30 a.m., five-and-twenty of those wonderful Uhlans . . . approached the celebrated Arc de Triomphe, and the leader, waving his sword, jumped the chain and took possession of Paris. Later, two thousand men, of all arms, came and held the Palais de l'Industrie and the Place de la Concorde, where French absurdity had veiled with black 'crepe' the faces of the 'Cities of France', which caused them exactly to resemble the widows of nigger melodists, and ridiculous enough to make an angel weep . . .

The event of today is too grave and too grand to realize at the moment. For hours the troops poured in . . .†

John Augustus O'Shea:

What a solid and stately array of puissant legions, the modern hammers of the earth, thundering by with gallant mien, their war-worn silken battle-flags waving over their heads! On they marched with steady ranks, strong, straight as spears, beaming with pride, for well nigh two hours – grenadiers, *jägers*, dragoons, lancers and giant cuirassiers – to spirit-stirring notes, clash of cymbal and beat of drum; and anon clattered past at a gallop a battery of field artillery. The spectacle was one of the most thrilling I had ever witnessed.‡

Felix Whitehurst:

Yes, it was a grand sight, a day of deep humiliation to France (though the Parisians seemed to like it so well that with another 'division' and half an hour's more music, they would have applauded), and a golden page in the history of Prussia, and I never was more weary or more sad.§

Dr Moritz Busch:

At dinner, . . . the Chief [Bismarck] told us he had ridden into Paris, and been recognised by the populace. No demonstration, however, had taken place against him. One person, who threw at him a very sinister glance, and up to whom he accordingly rode to ask for a light, readily complied with his request.*

Galignani's Messenger:

French troops were posted in the streets adjoining the Champs-Élysées, but evidently only for the purpose of preserving order, should their intervention be required. Everything was perfectly tranquil all over the city. No journals appeared, the proprietors having agreed during the enemy's stay to abstain from publication as a mark of public mourning.†

Édouard Thierry, Administrator-General of the Comédie-Française:

I stayed at home all day.

I was told that nearly all the shops were shut in the rue Saint-Antoine and the Boulevard Beaumarchais, with the following notice either printed or hand-written: 'Closed on account of public mourning.'

On the boulevard, the Garde nationale with piles of rifles . . .

M. de Bismarck is reported to have said that if there were an attempt to attack the Prussian troops, Paris would be burnt in three days.

I didn't hear the newsvendors' cries in the rue de Sully.

A workman came to clean the gas-jets on my staircase, but the gas wasn't lit this evening, either in the library or in the streets.

The rue de Sully is silent. No sound in the neighbouring streets or on the other side of the Seine.

The weather has remained magnificent.‡

That day, 1 March, the peace terms were ratified.

Next day, the subaltern in the Garde Landwehr was ordered to march,

with a number of non-commissioned officers, the so-called *Quartier-macher*, into Paris, and to wait at the Triumphal Arch for further orders, with a view to billeting the whole of our regiment for several days in Paris. I led my small detachment [he wrote] over the pontoon bridge by Suresnes, which was glorious with flags and flowers, and there I was once more within the Bois de Boulogne, which I had so often visited on former, happier occasions. Then – if the weather was as beautiful and springlike as on this 2 March – the park used to be thronged with glittering carriages, and gaily-dressed people on foot and on horseback. Today, the avenues, once so lovely, were filled with soldiers and with cannon. Alas for the stately avenues and the pleasant, shady walks! One almost fails to recognise them. The nearer you approach to Paris, the more you realise and shudder at the cruel havoc wrought by the pitiless axe. On the high road leading from the Triumphal Arch to the Grand Cascade, for a good quarter of an hour's walk, you see naught but the stumps of trees. The earthworks which had been thrown up, the barricades, etc., had been only in part removed, and as the troops were crowding in the narrow gaps or openings, it was only with difficulty that we could make our way to the arch.

What a fearful change – now and formerly!

Everywhere soldiers, batteries, horses unharnessed and drinking! Our guns turned their threatening mouths and gaping throats towards the Champs-Élysées, and at the first symptoms of resistance would have hurled death and destruction upon them. The large *reliefs* on the arch were covered with earth and planks as a protection against our bombs. On one of the protecting wooden walls the word 'Vengeance' was written in huge staring letters. In the avenues and side roads no restaurant – nay, not a single house – was open. On the Place de la Concorde the heads of the statues of the great cities of France were draped in black. The statue of Strasbourg was crowned with flowers. In the garden of the Tuileries, just beyond the line of demarcation, a few citizens, both male and female, were visible. They amused themselves by spitting fiercely on the ground, right before our men, and by behaving in so indecent a manner, that I must refrain from giving details.

The most warlike and, to me, most fascinating aspect was presented by the Place du Roi de Rome. Here a battalion of the 82nd Regiment of Infantry was bivouacking, and their picturesque straw huts extended to the bank of the Seine. Our batteries there 'covered' the Champ de Mars, where French National Guards were lying in their white tents. On the Pont de Jéna, Prussian soldiers were on guard on one side, French ones on the other. The day was clear and beautiful; the cupolas and towers glittered in the sunlight, and the stream which flowed on so quietly between friend and foe, was blue and glorious like the smiling sky above. The camp-fires, over which our men were preparing their meals, flickered most merrily. Officers and men were gaily strolling up and down, and the loud and mirthful music of the 82nd Regiment had actually the effect of alluring some Parisians, less obstinate than the rest, with a sprinkling of ladies even.*

At the musée du Louvre [recorded Édouard Thierry], the German officers went into the Galerie d'Apollon, which wasn't shut. The commanding officer at the Louvre had been ordered to padlock the windows, and he had not carried out the order. The officers opened them and came out on the balcony on the river side, facing the Garde nationale who were defending the entrance to the Pont des Arts. The same insolence, the same challenges. Some of the Gardes nationaux aimed at the enemy, and their officers had to rush in front of the rifles. Anyhow, the windows were shut at once. The commanding officer at the Louvre was dismissed . . .

The Prussians wanted to be quartered at the Austrian Embassy. The Ambassador declared that if they so violated the neutrality of his *hôtel* he would immediately ask for his passports.†

The aristocratic avenues 'du Roi de Rome' and 'de Josephine', glorious streets, broad and beautiful, and only laid out quite recently, had been assigned as quarters for our regiment [continued the subaltern in the Garde Landwehr], I had a most disagreeable and difficult task in billeting the men . . .

The task was not yet completed when an orderly galloped up to me with the official message that the Assembly at Bordeaux had accepted the conditions of peace, that the troops then quartered in Paris were to leave on the following morning, and that no further troops were to enter the city. Thus all my toil and trouble had been in vain; yet I do not regret this and am only glad that I have been able to spend a day – a memorable day – in Paris . . .

Not a single Parisian was amiable enough to sell us as much as a crust of bread. We hungered just as much as if it had been a regular fighting day. Still, I remained long in Paris with my little squad, rejoicing in the sight of the city, bathed in floods of silvery moonlight – rejoicing in the sight of such a mass of stalwart German soldiers thronging the Elysian Fields . . . It was near midnight when I led my men back to Mont Valérien. They were tired and hungry – these brave, truehearted, loyal men; but through the whole of the march home they were singing merrily, and the evergreen and beautiful patriotic songs of our native land resounded over the Bois de Boulogne.*

That day, Edward Blount, at the British Embassy, recorded:

Everything is as quiet as possible, but as long as the Prussians are here we are on a barrel of powder which the smallest spark may set fire to . . . The shops are all shut, the people all idle, and talking dreadful words: '*Nous ne sommes pas vaincus, mais vendus.*' '*Paris n'est pas pris.*' '*Les Prussiens ont peur,*' and the like. I suppose the Prussians will move off on Saturday, although they are in a position to do as they like . . . I am very anxious to get away, and hope to do so soon, but I cannot find out when Lord Lyons returns, and I must see him.†

Lord Lyons, the British Ambassador, was still at Bordeaux. That day he wrote to Lord Granville, the Foreign Secretary:

I suppose we may say peace at last . . .

How France is to be governed, and how the milliards are to be paid, are hard questions. The majority of the Assembly, which is decidedly anti-republican, hardly expects to establish a Government to its taste, without some actual fighting with the Reds in Paris and other large towns. It therefore does not at all like the idea of moving the Assembly to Paris. Thiers, I think, wishes to go to Paris . . . I cannot help thinking that the sooner the Government settles in the Capital, and has its fight (if fight there really must be) with the Mob over, the better.

As to what the new Government is to be, there would, with the present Assembly in its present mood, be, one would think, little difficulty in getting a large majority for a monarchy . . . Thiers, I believe, still thinks that for the present a Moderate Republic is the best compromise between all opinions, and the form of Government which least disunites Frenchmen.*

As for the Bonapartes, they were still detested. Princess Mathilde, the Emperor's cousin, was living in Brussels, and she was longing to return to Paris. Dumas *fils* dissuaded her.

2 March 1871

I'm back from Paris, I wanted to see – I've seen . . . I went through the most aristocratic and the most plebeian districts, for the moment you can't live in either. The scum are everywhere. Excitement, anger, vice, laziness, drunkenness, rancour, . . . ignorance and ineptitude at the bottom, powerlessness at the top. The vulgar herd, with all its traditional passions, is spreading over everything and covering the city like tainted oil. A Bonaparte, man or woman, however they behaved, would not only be insulted, but massacred, and a woman would run other risks as well. Nothing can give you an idea of this scum which is rising up from the very depths of society, . . . and showing all its old instincts, all the talons and teeth of '93 . . . If you want to keep the memory of Paris and the need to see it again, stay where you are. If you want to rid yourself of the idea for ever, without regrets and lamentations, go and spend forty-eight hours there, incognito, and look about you. You will take away such an impression of this heartrending spectacle that you won't even think about it again.

Show a little courage, Princess.*

Galignani's Messenger :

3 March

The Germans commenced their movement of evacuation at half past six in the morning in the midst of a thick fog, a party of Bavarians going first . . . Nearly all the enemy had gone by half-past nine, at which hour the sun had shone out brightly, showing an unclouded sky . . . When the last body had passed the circle around the Arc de Triomphe, cheering loudly for their Emperor as they passed beneath the splendid construction, a cordon of cavalry kept back the crowd with unnecessary violence. When at last the horsemen were obliged to advance, the spectators hissed and hooted them, and even some stones were thrown. At last, they followed the rest down the Avenue de la Grande-Armée, and the occupation of Paris was over . . . The occupation had lasted a little over forty-eight hours.†

Archibald Forbes:

I believe an extensive use is being made of Condy's disinfecting fluid and chloride of lime in the Palais de l'Industrie, the theatres on the Champs-Élysées, and other public buildings occupied by the Germans. Deodorizers had been largely strewn over the thoroughfares used by them, and the chain of enclosure around the Arc de Triomphe, over which the young hussar lieutenant had jumped his horse, had been removed and replaced. The original chain was no doubt being melted down into axles for dung-carts.‡

Flaubert to Princess Mathilde:

Saturday, 4 March

Well, it's over. The shame is swallowed, but it is not digested. How I thought of you on Wednesday, and how I suffered! All day I saw the Prussians' piles of arms shining in the sun in the Champs-Élysées, and I heard their music, their odious music blaring out under the Arc de Triomphe! The man who sleeps in the Invalides must be turning over in his tomb with rage!

What a world we are about to enter! Dumas, whom I saw yesterday, . . . told me that Paris was uninhabitable . . .*

Théophile Gautier to his daughter:

5 March

My dear darling,

. . . I am recovering slowly, though I had a slight relapse which set back my convalescence. I'm still coughing a great deal and I'm not very strong. Still I think that a few days hence I'll be in a state to take the train to Geneva, to come and kiss you after so long an absence, to hold you to my heart. How many terrible things have happened since the day I left you on the quayside at Chillon! It seems to me that ten years have passed. I've emerged all bruised from the rubble of events and I'm trying to piece the fragments of my broken life together. It isn't amusing, towards the end of one's career, after so much work and trouble – but it was written, as the Mussulman fatalists say. They're gradually taking the furniture back to the little house at Neuilly, and they're getting it ready as best they can to receive *its white angel*. But it's all a slow process. There are no more horses in Paris, they've all been eaten or very nearly. Here we are rid of the Prussians at last – my God, at what a cost! They made a not very brilliant entry followed by a prompt exit. When they reached the place de la Concorde, they found themselves face to face with the eight statues of the cities of France, stone spectres shrouded in black which waited for them in profound solitude. They did not dare to raise the crape veils. Nothing was more lugubrious and dreadful. The city is still incensed and trembling, but calm will come . . .

The author of your days
THÉOPHILE GAUTIER

12, rue de Beaune.†

Adolphe Thiers, who was now the head of the Executive Power, better understood the Parisian condition. On 6 March, from Bordeaux, he explained to the French Ambassador in London: 'The troubles in Paris are a nervous illness rather than anything else. I'm going to send reinforcements, and assemble 50,000 men there. This thought will soothe the nerves of some and prevent the villainy of others; or so I hope. If we have to fight, we shall fight.'*

Part Four

The Commune

The barrica

ussée Menilmontant

MARCH–MAY 1871

The National Assembly, now meeting at Bordeaux, was largely monarchist. Under the leadership of Thiers, they determined to eliminate the danger from the left, and now this virtually meant Paris. The Assembly was brought back from Bordeaux – not to Paris, but Versailles. Finally Thiers gave orders that the four hundred guns which were still in the hands of the National Guard in Paris were to be removed on 18 March. Thiers' order has been described as a delicate provocation; but he did not expect his troops from Versailles to fraternize with the Parisians He did expect the National Guard from the middle-class quarters of Paris to support him.

He had underestimated the effect of two measures passed by the Assembly. The first had ended the moratorium on the promissory notes through which much of the business of Paris was conducted; the second was to make rents which had remained unpaid during the war immediately payable. These decisions seemed very reasonable to him and to the landed gentry of the Assembly. They spelt ruin to the lower middle classes of Paris.

Thiers' attempted seizure of the guns was the spark which set off revolution in Paris. On Saturday, 18 March, Edwin Child recorded in his diary:

Revolution broke out, under the direction of a party calling themselves 'Comité Central', the pretext for it being the attempt on the part of the Government of Thiers to seize the cannons that have been guarded for some time past by the National Guards and which they claim as their own, saying that they were cast and paid for by the population and that therefore they by right belong to Paris and not to the army; this former an excuse but the real question at issue is 'capital & labour' the war cry being Commune and municipal rights, the motive power being the society called the International. The troops after being fired upon in the Place Pigalle, evacuated the town and retired to Versailles, the Government following shortly afterwards.*

*

At a moment of defeat and disillusionment, of lethargy and moral cowardice, the Communards showed vigour and courage; but they did not only number the courageous and even the patriotic; they gave all the disaffected and the disappointed, all the maladjusted and the frustrated a chance to indulge in licensed violence. On 18 March there came the first acts of senseless brutality. Clément Thomas, who had commanded the Garde nationale, and General Lecomte, whose troops had come to remove the guns, were captured by the rebels in Montmartre, and taken to a garden in the rue des Rosiers. There they were summarily shot. The anonymous author of *Paris-Commune* described how, as Clément Thomas came down the garden steps,

a shot rang out, and a bullet went through his cap. He was led to the garden wall, beside the peach-trees, on the left. In front of him was a platoon largely made up of sharpshooters and soldiers of the line, with a few National Guards mingled among them. An enormous crowd on every side; a great number of women. There were spectators all along the top of the garden walls. This throng of humanity demanded immediate execution.

The firing squad was commanded by a young lieutenant of the 169th battalion, a very gentle-looking man led by circumstances to take part in one of the most terrible deeds that popular movements can bring in their train.

Clément Thomas, very pale, took off his cap; he wanted to speak, but he was choked by emotion. Before the order to fire was given, a shot rang out. Clément Thomas fell, face to the ground. The shooting continued . . .

General Lecomte was pushed beside the body of General Clément Thomas . . .

They fired at him. He fell on his back . . .

After the crowd had dispersed, quite a number of sightseers, brought there by the shots, came into the garden to stare at the corpses.*

Mrs Moulton, an American socialite, was staying at Petit Val: on her breakfast tray, with her tea and buttered toast, she found a note from her husband announcing that Paris was once again under arms.

A revolution (*rien que ça*) had broken out [she wrote to her mother], and all approaches to the city were barricaded. This was news indeed! I understood why no carriage came last night, why trains were stopped, why telegraph wires were cut, and why no mother-in-law appeared...

But, as the Psalmist puts it, 'Sorrow endureth for a night, but joy cometh in the morning.' My joy came late in the afternoon, on returning from a drive to Petit Val, where I found the landau of the American Legation, my mother-in-law, and . . . the American Minister himself, the popular and omnipotent Mr Washburne.

They were overjoyed to see me, as they had been as anxious as I had been, having tried every means in their power to reach me. To telegraph was impossible; to send a groom on horseback equally so. Finally, as a last resource, they had written to Mr Washburne to see if he could not solve the difficult question, which he did by driving out himself with Mrs Moulton to fetch me.

As soon as the horses were sufficiently rested, . . . we started for Paris, passing through Alfort, Charenton, and many villages, all more or less in ruins. There were plenty of people lounging about in the streets. We reached Vincennes without difficulty; but thenceforth our troubles commenced in earnest.

Mr Washburne thought it more prudent to close the carriage, cautioning the coachman to drive slower. We were stopped at every moment by soldiers and barricades; then Mr Washburne would show his card and his *laissez passer*, after which we were allowed to pass on, until we came to more soldiers and more barricades. Omnibuses turned over, paving-stones piled up, barrels, ladders, ropes stretched across the streets, anything to stop the circulation. Poor Mr Washburne was tired out popping his head first out of one window then out of the other, with his card in his hand.

The men who accosted us were not discourteous, but spoke quite decidedly, as if they did not expect to be contradicted. We did not care to contradict them, either.

'We know you, Monsieur, by reputation, and we know that you are well disposed towards France. How do you feel towards *la Commune*?'

Mr Washburne hesitating a moment, the man added, cynically, 'Perhaps you would like to add a stone to our barricades.' He made as if he would open the door of the carriage; but Mr Washburne answered, holding back the door, 'I take it for granted, Monsieur, that I have your permission to drive on, as I have something very important to attend to at my Legation,' and gave the man a defiant look, which rather frightened him, and we drove through the crowd. All along the rue de Rivoli we saw the soldiers massing together in groups, *la Garde nationale* (Mr Washburne said they so called themselves since yesterday), a miserable-looking set of men, talking very loud and flourishing their guns as if they were walking-sticks.

This was a sight to behold! The space around the Column was filled with paving-stones and all sorts of débris (strange to say, my eyes saw more brooms than anything else); and cannon pointing everywhere. A very impertinent, common-looking *voyou* said, on looking at Mr Washburne's card, 'Vous êtes tous très chic, . . . mais vous ne passerez pas, tout de même.'

We shook in our shoes.

But Mr Washburne, equal to the occasion, said something which had the desired effect, and we passed on . . .

I could have cried when I saw the Tuileries; it was only last August I had had a delightful half-hour with the Empress (she asked me to take tea with her). Then she was full of confidence in the triumph of the Emperor (who could have doubted it?), pleased that her son should have received the *baptême du feu*, as the Emperor telegraphed – oh, the pity of it all! and that was only last August – seven months ago.*

Lord Lyons to Lord Granville:

Paris, 20 March

We are in a strange state indeed. How it will end, who shall say? The Prussians may be glad of a chance to wipe away the absurdity of their three days' occupation by a more serious entrance, and it may suit their rulers to put down Belleville, with a view to checking the progress of Republicanism. I should think however it would be wiser of them, with their hatred of France, to leave the Parisians to accomplish their own ruin.

A good many National Guards have gone out towards Versailles, whether with the view of making a serious attack on the Government and the Assembly remains to be seen. It seems to be doubtful whether there are any troops, except perhaps the Papal Zouaves, on whom the Government can depend . . .

It is to be hoped that the Assembly will not make matters worse by violent and ill-considered resolutions. I suppose it will be furious with Thiers for having brought it to Versailles, and it is on the cards that it may be really attacked there today by the Parisians. Any way, I should not be at all surprised if the Assembly transferred itself to some dismal French provincial town.*

The Assembly remained in Versailles; and on 26 March Paris went to the polls. Its new municipal council was controlled by Reds in a proportion of four to one, and they promptly assumed the title, with its threatening Jacobin overtones, of Commune de Paris.

Théophile Gautier to Carlotta Grisi:

Versailles, Saturday 25, March 1871

My dear Carlotta,

The papers have no doubt told you about the horrible things which are happening. My trunk was packed, and I was going to leave, but instead of going to Geneva I had 'to fall back in good order' on Versailles, which is now the capital of France since Paris is in the power of the insurgents . . . We thought that we had reached the bottom of the gulf, but there are spirals still to be descended. What grief at the end of a life of so much toil, a life built up with such labour, to see everything crumble about you and to be crushed in a heap of ruins! How sad it is to be far from your family and still to consider yourself fortunate that they are not there in the whirlwind of calamities!*

Queen Victoria's journal:

Windsor Castle, 27 March 1871

At a little before three, went down with our children and Ladies and Gentlemen to receive the Emperor Napoleon. I went to the door with Louise and embraced the Emperor '*comme de rigueur*'. It was a moving moment, when I thought of the last time he came here in '55, in perfect triumph, dearest Albert bringing him from Dover, the whole country mad to receive him, and now! He seemed much depressed and had tears in his eyes, but he controlled himself and said, '*Il y a bien longtemps que je n' ai vu votre Majesté.*' He led me upstairs and we went into the Audience Room. He is grown very stout and grey and his moustaches are no longer curled or waxed as formerly, but otherwise there was the same pleasing, gentle, and gracious manner. My children came in with us. The Emperor at once spoke of the dreadful and disgraceful state of France, and said that all that had passed during the last few months had greatly lowered the French character ... There seemed to be '*point d'énergie*'. He was dreadfully shocked at '*tout ce qui se passe à Paris*'.†

Next day, 28 March, the Commune officially installed itself at the Hôtel de Ville in Paris. In *My Adventures in the Commune*, Ernest Vizetelly recorded:

The Commune was formally proclaimed on the Place de l'Hôtel-de-Ville, which was then crowded with National Guards and spectators. As the sight of a monarch would have been offensive, the equestrian bas-relief of Henry of Navarre above the entrance to the municipal building was covered with red drapery, more of which decorated a stand on which the members both of the Commune and of the Central Committee took their places.

Few of them were good-looking, but they had exerted themselves to appear imposing. The members of the Commune wore red scarves with gold tassels, and red rosettes with pendant ribbons fringed with gold; whilst the Committee men had red scarves with silver fringe, and triangular decorations hanging from red and black ribbons. Many of them, of course, were in uniform as officers of the National Guard, and seemed to be very proud of all the gold braid which decorated their sleeves. Speeches were made, the election returns as published in the *Journal Officiel* were read aloud, an artillery salute was fired, the National Guards hoisted their *képis* on their bayonets and shouted 'Vive la Commune!' till they were hoarse, whereupon bands of music struck up in turn the 'Marseillaise', the 'Chant du Départ', and the 'Chant des Girondins'. There had been some talk of issuing an edict to compel people to illuminate their residences that evening, but for one or another reason the idea was abandoned. The illuminations were reserved for a later date – when the palaces of Paris blazed on both sides of the Seine.*

That day, writing from Versailles, the American Minister reported:

Lord Lyons made an early call on me. He considers the situation as bad as possible. The truth is, the government has not sufficient force to undertake operations. Thiers told his lordship last night that it would be three weeks before they would have an army strong enough to attack the insurgents. Jules Favre thinks that when they get that force the insurgents in Paris will cave in. He is mistaken . . .†

Lord Lyons to Lord Granville:

Versailles, 30 March 1871
The Commune are going ahead in Paris. The great comfort the Government and the Assembly here have, is that the similar movements in other great towns have failed, and that thus it is plainly Paris against all France. Their great hope appears to be that the members of the Commune will quarrel among themselves, and that their social measures may be so thoroughly socialist, as to rouse resistance among the

Parisians. In the meantime however the delay seems dangerous; the working classes are said to be going over more and more completely to the Commune, and the effect of a completely successful revolution in Paris on the other towns may yet be serious. Bismarck is said to have given Thiers a limited time (a fortnight or three weeks) to set things straight, and to have declared that, when that time is up, the Germans must step in.*

Mr Washburne:

Versailles, 31 March

Have just returned from a reception of M. Thiers. His residence is at the Prefecture of the Department of the Seine et Oise, which is really a large and beautiful palace. It was the residence of the King of Prussia while he was in Versailles. There was quite a large number of people present, nearly all gentlemen; only about half a dozen ladies. Everybody seemed desirous of talking with M. Thiers and giving him advice. There is much complaint in respect to his policy. He answers that he did not seek his position and would be very glad to give it up; that while he holds it he will act according to his own judgment. He says he is doing his best in his own way and that he works twenty hours a day. Perhaps he may stretch that a little, but he has always been a great worker. For a man seventy-four years of age he is wonderfully bright and active, and tough as a pine-knot. He always gets up at four o'clock in the morning; but then he sleeps an hour before dinner and an hour after. He has his own theories and is impatient under any criticism. He asked me about Paris, and I told him that things were growing worse and worse there all the time, a proposition which he warmly contradicted, and declared that things were getting better and better all the time. Differing so completely, I thought it useless to continue the conversation with him on that subject. There are seventy thousand troops in and about Versailles and the government persists [*sic*] that they cannot be depended upon, and they are waiting for other troops to come. If any man wants to be disgusted, let him come to Versailles.†

Rev. William Gibson, Wesleyan Minister:

Paris, 31 March

I have just learned that no letters have entered Paris this morning, and that the gates are shut. The trains are stopped on some of the lines. So we are shut up as in a cage! As I went out our *concierge* said, 'I never felt afraid, but now I am trembling . . .'

Evening

As we are shut in, I thought it would be well to lay in a stock of provisions, and went this afternoon to Potin's, a large provision merchant. The shop was crowded with people on the same errand with myself, and I had difficulty in getting served. One poor woman near me said, '*C'est le dernier jour de notre vie.*'*

Unlike Lord Lyons and Mr Washburne, Thiers remained convinced that time was on his side. On 6 April he replaced General Vinoy, his commander, by Marshal MacMahon, who was eager to make amends for the humiliation of Sedan. Favre was sent to Prussian headquarters to obtain permission to increase the French regular Army beyond the limits prescribed in the Peace Treaty. Bismarck was now beginning to fear the impact which the Commune might have on the Socialists in Germany. He readily agreed that the Army might be increased – ultimately to 170,000 men. Four hundred thousand prisoners of war were speedily sent home to France, to be rehabilitated and then prepared to lay siege to Paris. There could be no serious attempt to re-enter Paris until the *Versaillais* were organized; but Thiers kept up the pressure on the suburb of Neuilly. The bridge was recaptured, but for most of April the fighting was to continue from street to street.

Lili Gautier stubbornly lived in the cellar in the rue de Longchamp. Gautier and his other sister, Zoé, tried to settle at Versailles, but they could not rest. On 6 April Gautier wrote to his daughter Estelle, in Switzerland:

3, avenue de Saint-Cloud,
Versailles

Dear darling,

   ... Here we are engaged in civil war, and we are going to lay siege
to Paris. There is really a spirit of madness throughout our country.
Even the wise are forced by the mad into extravagant acts. In the
meanwhile it is the most unbearable life you could imagine. All day
long you are on the alert, listening to the cannon, the shooting nearer
or farther away, discussing the occasional news that arrives from Paris
and crosses the lines. You snatch the papers from the vendors' hands,
and walk up and down in front of the Hôtel des Réservoirs and the
Assemblée Nationale to watch for the coming and going of deputies
to pick up some odd scraps of information. Nothing is more ener-
vating. The posts to Paris and the suburbs are no longer running, and
we know nothing of the destiny of friends who could not escape or
didn't believe such disorders were possible. The letters for Geneva
are taken by courriers at Fontainebleau station, and that is how we
can correspond. It is the same for other destinations. They've been
fighting at Courbevoie and the Pont de Neuilly ... Our house was
untouched. We were all three of us at Versailles and Lili, who'd
walked from Neuilly, had crossed the bridge an hour beforehand with
no idea that in a few minutes it would become a battlefield. We are
regretting the time of the siege when at least there was hope. Until
now the party of order is in control – outside Paris, of course, for in
Paris there is the most complete anarchy. The troops did not raise
their rifle butts as the rioters hoped, and they are fighting on both
sides with a ferocity which they would have done better to use against
the Prussians. The attempts of the Reds to take Versailles have failed.
They were beaten, and they lost two or three thousand prisoners.
But Paris must be entered. That is the difficulty when you don't want
to destroy everything with fire and sword. Such, my poor darling, is
the life your poor father leads so far away from you. I'm always held
back as I'm about to leave, and I'm bursting with spleen and rage.
Yet I hope that one of these days I shall come to occupy the little

room at 40 francs a month that you've found for me, and spend three
or four weeks with you. I need it after the hardships I have suffered
... I kiss you a thousand times, and Carlotta and Ernestine. The aunts
follow suit ...

Your father,
THÉOPHILE GAUTIER*

Ernest A. Vizetelly:

On the morning of 6 April I was by chance present at a strange
spectacle on what was for a long time called the Place du Prince
Eugène, but is now the Place Voltaire. A statue of the great French
writer and philosopher was already there at the time of the Commune,
and for this reason the spot was deemed an appropriate one for the
destruction of the guillotine. At that period executions took place
publicly on the Place de la Roquette, and the so-called *bois de justice*
were kept in a kind of shed in the Rue de la Folie-Regnault. Thither
that morning, at a very early hour, repaired a band of zealous National
Guards and others who speedily forced the door of the storeplace
and carried the various sections of the apparatus into the street,
whence they removed them to the open space in front of the statue
of Voltaire. Some delay then ensued, presumably in order that the
Commune's full authority for the destruction of the guillotine might
be obtained. At all events, the bonfire was not lighted until about
ten o'clock, and when by chance I reached the scene half an hour
later, the hated 'instrument of justice' was already partially consumed.
The delight of the crowd at this unexpected *auto-da-fe* was manifest.
To hear folks talk one might have thought the death-penalty for ever
abolished; but, as Rochefort very sensibly remarked in *Le Mot
d'Ordre*, what was the use of destroying the guillotine merely to replace it by guns? ...

From the Place Voltaire I repaired to Père-Lachaise to witness the
funeral of some thirty unrecognised Communards who had fallen
in the recent fighting ... Seven members of the Commune, all of
them wearing their red scarves fringed with gold, attended this first

solemn funeral of the unknown victims of the civil war. There were three vehicles, each carrying some ten coffins. A military band was in attendance, and there was naturally a numerous escort of Guards, with *immortelles* in their gun-barrels. The procession came by way of the principal boulevards as far as the Château d'Eau (now Place de la République) and then turned into the Boulevard Voltaire, passing on its way the ashes of the departed guillotine. At the graveside Delescluze, who was no mean speaker, delivered an oration.

Day by day, Paris was becoming more and more deserted. The hostages decree was of a nature to alarm all people of any prominence, and particularly the clergy, as the Communalist press declared that at least five hundred priests ought to be imprisoned. Young men, moreover, found themselves confronted by Cluseret's decree that all who were between the ages of seventeen and thirty-five should be enrolled in the National Guard. In one or other connection not a day elapsed without several arrests. An order went forth to imprison M. Groult, a famous maker of *pâtes alimentaires*, and, as he could not be found, it was declared that his wife and children should be apprehended unless he paid a fine of 100,000 francs. Henri Vrignault, editor of *Le Bien Public*, was also 'wanted', but contrived to make his escape. Richardet, of *Le National*, was arrested on applying for a passport to leave Paris. Paul Dupont, the eminent printer, was sought for, but happened to be already at Versailles. Lacroix, the well-known publisher of many of Victor Hugo's works, and the traffic-manager of the Western Railway Line were less fortunate. Further, a fresh raid was made on Peters's Restaurant, now the Café Américain, on the Boulevards, in the hope of apprehending a large number of 'reactionaries' at one swoop. Among the priests who were incarcerated were the septuagenarian Abbé Deguerry, Curé of the Madeleine, whose house was entered and plundered at dead of night, the Curés of Saint-Séverin, Saint-Laurent, and Montmartre, and the director of the Seminary of Saint-Sulpice ...

Meantime the hunt for refractory Guards continued on all sides. Several of the Paris butchers, however, protested so vigorously against their assistants being taken away – threatening, if that were done, to close their shops and sell no meat – that it was decided to dispense journeymen-butchers from service in the Guard. Some similar arrangement was arrived at respecting the bakers, for the Citizen-Members of the Commune had no desire to be starved. However, they sent some of their myrmidons to the asylum of La Salpêtrière, and forced all the young men employed there, to join the National Guard. And still and ever the exodus from Paris continued. A good many young fellows let themselves down from the ramparts at night by means of ropes. Others dressed themselves up as girls, and . . . they were sometimes detected and marched off in their petticoats to a guard-house. Older people besieged the Prefecture of Police for passports. There were long queues of them as well as scores of waiting vehicles around the statue of Desaix on the old Place Dauphine.*

Rev. William Gibson:

7 April

We are truly again in the 'Reign of Terror'. Many have been arrested and imprisoned, and there is a general feeling of uneasiness throughout the city. The guillotine was set up on the Boulevard Voltaire, but it was immediately burned, and I hear two accounts, one that it was burned by the indignant people, another that it was brought out from the prison de la Roquette and burned purposely to show the people's horror of capital punishment. There was heavy fighting in the direction of Courbevoie yesterday morning and afternoon. There was a terrible fusillade on the bridge of Neuilly, and the bridge and barricade are both now in the hands of the Versailles troops . . . A National Guard said today, '*Nous serons bientôt écrasés.*'†

Fidus: *La Révolution de septembre* :

Étampes, 9 April

A decree of the Commune obliges all men from nineteen to forty to join the combat units. It has terrified people; it's a question of who won't obey and who will escape, and every means of leaving Paris is tried. One learns from those who have managed to escape by what manifold, ingenious, bizarre, even comical means they have avoided the fierce vigilance of the Commune guards. The youngest, disguised as women, and wearing thick black veils, their faces covered with rice-powder, pass without difficulty; others put on a waggoner's smock, and, whip in hand, go out behind a waggon which easily gets through the gates. At the beginning there were some who piously followed a funeral as far as the cemetery outside the walls (near the Maison-Blanche), and then escaped. However, this fraud was soon discovered: funerals were then escorted by National Guards who obliged all the mourners to return to Paris . . .

This general flight, in which everything is abandoned, house, business, fortune, interests, friendships, affections: this flight in which, with one accord, people only seek to save their lives, is comment enough on the situation in Paris.*

Captain Hozier:

Another cause of intense terror and suffering was the domiciliary visits of the National Guards; these had a dual object, the finding of arms, and also of National Guards, or of any able-bodied men, in hiding. Woe to any who were found, especially in uniform; they were immediately marched off to the forts or the advanced posts, and their chance of escape was small. Every kind of weapon that was found was taken away; and when the house or apartment belonged to a late senator or other marked Bonapartist, all the valuables were seized, and frequently the furniture and other things destroyed.†

An inhabitant of Neuilly:

10 April

Impossible to go out. The butcher and the baker came at five o'clock this morning to bring provisions for two days. The shooting begins at about six o'clock and it never stops . . .

We are sleeping in the cellar.

A man tried to cross the avenue, and he was fatally wounded.‡

Ernest A. Vizetelly:

The German bombardment of Paris did some little damage to property, and resulted in the death of a hundred and the wounding of about two hundred people. Its effect was absolutely trivial in comparison with the destruction and the loss of life occasioned by the French bombardment of the capital. The number of victims was then at least eight times as large, and the damage to buildings was infinitely more severe. During the German Siege, moreover, the western districts of Paris had remained virtually immune, protected as they were by Mont Valérien; but now they were being bombarded by the batteries installed in that fortress and on other positions, and suffered far more than the southern districts, for instance, had suffered from the German fire a few months previously . . .

Skirmishing went on in the Bois as well as in the streets and gardens of Neuilly, under the bright spring sky and amidst all the young blossoms and fresh green foliage. In vain did the scent of the lilac-bushes strive to contend with the smell of powder. It was the latter which the mild April breezes wafted incessantly hither and thither, whilst clouds of smoke enveloped each budding plant like deadly blight.

The firing still continued at night time, when on either side small parties of men went prowling about, but were often fired upon from some shuttered window or loopholed wall. If the Government troops were in a difficult position, some of the Communalists were almost in jeopardy, for although they still held the village of Asnières it seemed as if they might be cut off from Paris by the detachments of soldiers scouring Neuilly on the one hand and Levallois-Perret on the other. A good many of the residents of these localities, who had hidden themselves away in their cellars, were still there, in semi-obscurity and a state of semi-starvation, not daring to venture forth in search of food, which, moreover, they might not have been able to procure as every shop was closed.

The 11th of April was a quieter day than the preceding ones. The

Communalists were busy installing heavy guns on the Trocadéro, whence they hoped to be able to fire on Mont Valérien . . .*

Edwin Child to 'W. H. Child, 43, Worship St., Finsbury, London, Angleterre':

11 April

Dear Father,

. . . What a disgrace for poor France, almost ruined by an implacable enemy, and now brought to the verge of destruction by its own children, somebody is to blame but who ? It is just as difficult for the troops to get in as it was for the Prussians, notwithstanding that they hold the Mont Valérien. As for these Communists they are a set of madmen nothing better, they would stand at nothing, all that they desire is a fair share of power and plunder, and the rest they leave to chance, no respectable battalion will fight for them, a few guard the public buildings but the fighting they leave to Montmartre and Belleville and the more these two suffer in dead and wounded the better for the nation. At one time I was almost French in sentiment, but I now scorn them almost as much as I do Germans. When an enormous majority of respectable citizens such as in Paris at the moment, allow themselves to be governed and even commanded by such a set as now in power, I say that they are not worthy of the pity of any respectable man, the insurgents, taking a most liberal estimate, are not more than 100,000 strong, leaving upwards of 220,000 orderly citizens *armed* to put them down with a regular army to back them, they are a d – n – d set of cowardly fools. At the present moment it is impossible for those in Paris to do anything, but at the commencement if the people had moved, all this bloodshed might have been averted, but no, every man had some excuse, one had his shop, another his wife, another didn't hold with civil war, another didn't want to pay his rent and so on till a row became a revolution and the words Liberty, Fraternity & Égalité, mean obedience to our orders (Commune), pillage of all churches, and fighting against your own brother, . . . & all this from the madness of the Commune, & the stubbornness of the National Assembly. This is the fruits of Trochu, Jules Favre, & Co's

Inflating a balloon outside the Hôtel de Ville

The hospital in the Theâtre-Français

government, had they employed these ruffians against the Prussians a different tale might have been told about the war and this additional disgrace to the country would never have happened. Fancy, Paris *asking* the Prussians to protect them, and yet people talk about it coolly enough now & their entry would be hailed by many with pleasure, I am getting heartily sick of the country & its inhabitants ...

Have no fears as regards my safety & with love to all I remain,

Yours,

EDWIN*

Ernest A. Vizetelly:

It rained rather heavily on the evening of 11 April, and it was under a dark, heavy, lowering sky that firing was resumed from nine until eleven o'clock. That very day, I believe, MacMahon had assumed active command of the Versailles army. The artillery of Cissey's corps cannoned Forts Issy and Vanves vigorously. An attempt was also made to seize the Communalist positions in advance of Montrouge, but this was repulsed. The people, who, in palmy days of peace, had set up telescopes in one or another Parisian square and charged the public ten centimes apiece for a brief inspection of the beauties of Venus or the moon, and who afterwards, during the first siege, had turned their lenses upon the German positions around Paris, were now showing us the Versaillese batteries; and many sight-seers repaired to the Point-du-Jour viaduct in order to take a peep at the guns which were cannonading Issy, Vanves, and Passy ...

The Government troops had entrenched themselves as best they could in the positions which they held at Neuilly, the recapture of which suburb became the paramount desire of the Communalists. The first attempt which Dombrowski made with that object early on the morning of 12 April, did not succeed; but reinforcements reached him during the afternoon, and the regular army then had to seek cover in the Bois de Boulogne. The various barricades and earth-works which the troops had thrown up, were seized by the Communalists and utilized by them ...

At a very early hour on the following morning the troops were put to the task of recapturing Neuilly. A fierce fight went on there all day . . . *

An inhabitant of Neuilly:

13 April

I want to go to my office in Paris, but I cannot cross the avenue . . . The federates have taken the offensive again, and the bullets are humming about like cockchafers.

At about eleven o'clock, another shell splinter comes through the attic roof, and rebounds under the rinsing tub. This fragment weighs 650 grammes. At two o'clock, a smaller splinter falls in the middle of the courtyard.

The grocer has no more sugar, tobacco or flour. The butcher hasn't come, and all I have been able to find is bread.†

Ernest A. Vizetelly:

With only a couple of railway lines remaining to supply our needs, the prices of provisions rose throughout Paris, and I remember that, about the middle of April, horse-flesh – virtually banished from our tables since the German siege – again appeared in some of the butchers' shops. At one corner of the Rue de la Paix and the Place Vendôme there was an English establishment where tea was sold, and one day, in order to make some purchases, I managed to get through the cordon of Guards stationed at this point. I was then able to survey the barricades defending the Place Vendôme and the many little tents which had been pitched there, and which gave the square the appearance of a veritable bivouac. Women, provided with coffee-cans or selling flowers, were going hither and thither among the National Guards, with whom they laughed and chatted. There was as yet no sign of the demolition of the Vendôme column. Yellow wreaths of immortelles, offered by the veterans of the Invalides at the last Fête Napoléon, still hung from the railings by which the column was encompassed. The latter's destruction, however, was merely delayed, and one morning the *Journal Officiel* issued an announcement inviting tenders for two lots of building materials and two lots of metal, forming part of the monument of *la grande armée.**

Rev. William Gibson:

Several shells have struck the Arc de Triomphe, occasioning, however, but little damage. The statues representing the principal French towns in the Place de la Concorde still keep the black covering over their faces. They may well mourn over poor France . . . With the return of spring might have come the return of happiness and prosperity were it not for these internal discords. Alas! When will they cease? From much that I have seen and heard I am forced to the conclusion that many of these fellows of Belleville and Montmartre, finding themselves with arms in their hands, are determined to go on with the game of fighting, and, other enemies failing, no matter to them, they will fight their own countrymen. Many of them know not what they are fighting for. I don't wonder that just now so many French are ashamed of their nationality.†

18 April

The more I get to know about this insurrectionary movement, the more I am convinced that it is a great effort of the Red Republican party in Europe to gain their ends. They have been on the look-out for years for a field of operations; they could not find it in England or Germany, but in Paris, at this particular juncture, they have found exactly what they have long wanted. And to make their cause more popular they have turned the legitimate desire on the part of the Parisians, to have the municipal management of Paris in their own hands, to suit their own nefarious purposes. Two entirely distinct things have been blended together. Hence Paris gets blame which she does not deserve. The Assembly is angry at Paris. The country complains of Paris. The anger and complaint should be directed against that which Paris happens to contain at the present moment. The 'word of order' to these people in Paris is said to come from the International Society in London! These are questions in which all Europe is interested. Unfortunately poor Paris has to suffer because she is the scene of strife. The scum of Europe has been collected here in Paris to fight out this battle. I have never seen such countenances, not even typified in Madame Tussaud's Chamber of Horrors, as are now to be seen in Paris.*

Théophile Gautier to his daughter:

> *3, avenue de Saint-Cloud,*
> *Versailles*
> *19 April 1871*

Dear darling,

Some very terrible things have happened since my last letter. Courbevoie and the bridge at Neuilly have become the scenes of bitter fighting. The avenue is constantly being swept by the combatants' cannon, mitrailleuses and howitzers. Lili, seeing peace restored after several days, had the unfortunate idea of going back to the house, where she has found herself blockaded and is living in the cellar like the whole population of Neuilly. As you can imagine, we have been dreadfully anxious. It is impossible to go and join her or to make her turn back to Versailles. All the lines are cut and anyone who tried to cross them would be exposed to the fire of the besiegers and the besieged. For a whole week, we did not know if she was alive or dead, buried under the débris of the house. She finally found a means, no doubt by some soldiers returning to Versailles, of getting some letters to us and reassuring us about herself. The last of them arrived yesterday, 18 April. Lili is very well, the house hasn't been damaged, seriously at least, because I couldn't answer for a few bullets lost in the walls. This life of anxiety and dispersion is unbearable. One is mortally bored at Versailles; copy isn't accepted because of the Chambers, which fill all the paper. Money is getting low, and one doesn't know how to replace it. It's very sad. The *communeux* aren't as nice as you imagine them to be in Switzerland. The Republic is certainly very fine as long as it remains a theory, but with us when they try to put it into practice it immediately turns into civil war. The role of a prophet of doom doesn't attract me, but you must remember that in my letters, for more than two months, I have been predicting days worse than the June days after the February Revolution in 1848. A real Terror is reigning in Paris as in '93. They have burnt the guillotine, it's true; but the chassepot rifle replaces it to advantage. Six hundred thousand people have left Paris, the streets are deserted, the shops are shut or only half open. People escape by slipping down a knotted rope from the top of the ramparts, but you must see all that in the papers . . . Rest assured that as soon as I can I shall come and embrace you all . . .

Your father

THÉOPHILE GAUTIER*

Mr Washburne:

All is one great shipwreck in Paris. Fortune, business, public and private credit, industry, labour, are all 'in the deep bosom of the ocean buried'. The physiognomy of the city becomes every day more sad. All the upper part of the Champs-Élysées is completely deserted for fear of the shells. Immense barricades are going up at the Place de la Concorde. The great manufactories and workshops are closed; the vast magazines, where are to be found all the wonders and marvels of Parisian industry, are no longer open, the cafés close at ten o'clock, and Paris is not Paris when the cafés are shut up. Where I write (No. 75, Avenue Uhrich), always the roar of cannon, the whizzing of shells and the rattling of musketry.†

Lord Lyons to Lord Granville:

Versailles, 21 April 1871

I suppose we shall get back to Paris, or to the ruins of it, some day; and certainly the affairs of the Commune are looking more gloomy than they did, but I must leave to Thiers the responsibility of the perpetually renewed declaration that we shall be there in a few days. The sooner it comes the better, for the delay is very dangerous for Thiers himself and for the country. The great towns in the south will hardly be kept under if Paris remains in rebellion much longer, and Thiers will find it very difficult to hold back the monarchical majority in the Assembly.‡

Théophile Gautier to Carlotta Grisi:

21 April

I hasten to answer your kind, good letter. Perhaps tomorrow the railways will no longer be working. All the communications between Paris and Versailles are cut, and they expect a big battle tomorrow or the day after . . . These gentlemen seem to forget that the Prussians still occupy our country and are moving back towards Paris. The papers don't reach us any more from the capital, and they are printed at Versailles. Journalists are sentenced to death, printing works shut down and sacked, banks are robbed, food requisitioned, and without being a pessimist one may be allowed not to see the future in bright colours. We are going towards '93 and the Terror; only there won't be a guillotine. They will hack people to pieces and shoot them in the street without any form of trial: that's what they call liberty in France! The red flag . . . is floating over the Hôtel de Ville and all the dishonoured monuments of Paris.*

Edwin Child:

24 April

Dear Mother,

I daresay you feel very uneasy about me in all these riots or rather in this revolution but there is nothing to fear, I go quietly about what I have to do & trouble nobody & nobody troubles me.

All my friends and acquaintances, with one exception, have left Paris, and I'm quite alone, without being lonely. Food so far is not in any way scarce but meat is dear 2/6d a lb but then it always is in Paris compared with London. I have laid in this time 3 or 4 large boxes of biscuits, concentrated milk, jam etc. and so if by misfortune we should have to sustain another siege I can laugh at them . . .

Both sides are much to blame, but right is right, & Versailles instead of making up for lost time simply wades deeper in the mud. I went to Versailles last Wednesday, and got arrested 5 times, . . . but at last arrived safely . . .

With love to all,
EDWIN†

On 25 April, Thiers agreed to the request of the Commune for an armistice at Neuilly, in order to allow the evacuation of the wretched and half-starved inhabitants. By now there was hardly a house left standing in the village, and many of its residents were almost too weak to leave their cellars.

Ernest A. Vizetelly:

The quietude which suddenly prevailed appeared to be the greater as it was so very unusual. One missed that constant booming of guns which on other days made itself heard so frequently and ominously above every other sound of the city's feverish life.

Now neither the thunder of artillery nor the crepitation of musketry was to be heard, whilst people hastily flocked to the Champs-Élysées, the Avenue de la Grande Armée and the Avenue des Ternes, all eager to witness the removal of the remaining unfortunate denizens of Neuilly and Les Ternes, and, if possible, to obtain a glimpse of the destruction said to have been wrought beyond the ramparts by the cannonading of recent weeks. On crossing the Place de l'Étoile I observed that here and there the Arc de Triomphe was slightly damaged; and as I went down the Avenue de la Grande Armée the traces of the bombardment became more and more numerous. Several houses, particularly some near the Rue Rude, were ruins. Great branches of trees, carried away by passing projectiles, lay upon the ground. Every now and then, too, a broken street-lamp was stretched across the footway. Beyond the Porte-Maillot, the so-called Château de l'Étoile, a former *brasserie*, was still standing. Of recent years it had been used by an English importing firm as a store-place for Bass's ale, Guinness's stout, Crosse and Blackwell's pickles, and so forth. Along the Boulevard d'Inkermann and the Avenue des Ternes one was again confronted by abundant destruction. Rescued people were being placed – often with some of their goods and chattels – in vehicles of various kinds, which, heavily laden, went slowly into Paris; and at intervals you saw, in some corner or other, a dead body over which flies were constantly hovering and buzzing.*

Under cover of the twelve-hour truce, Thiers disengaged the weight of his artillery from the Neuilly sector and transferred it to the sector facing Issy-les-Moulineaux. Fifty-three batteries of guns were mustered there, supported by powerful infantry contingents. Next day Thiers announced the opening of 'active operations'.

Lili Gautier to her brother:

Neuilly, 29 April

My dear Théo we are still in the cellar as you can well imagine the days are long but what can you do when the madmen are let loose *the sane* like ourselves aren't happy they talk of a vote which would settle matters let's hope that it will end one day, it is very sad not to be able to breathe because of a handful of scoundrels old Robelin is walking like a cat through the shells you are well that's what matters to me most Zoé is becoming a heroine as for me I am very well I'm quite well [*sic*] I'm coughing but that's the cellar I'm ending my letter Monsieur Robelin is snatching it away I kiss you most affectionately my very best wishes to Estelle and to dear Carlotta I think that you receive news Zoé must go and walk little Zizi [the dog] because he likes a walk very much take care of yourself as much as you can and Zoé mustn't take risks *shells* are bad jokes

Most affectionately L.G.*

On 30 April, the fort of Issy was evacuated. It was the worst military blow to befall the Commune. By this time, Thiers had also organized an effective blockade of food supplies to Paris, and the Prussians were co-operating on their side of the city.

Lili Gautier to her brother:

Neuilly,
6 May

My dear Théo we are still the same oh when will this stupid war end the world is growing madder and madder where is it leading who knows the leaders always make us hope that it will end in three or four days and it has now been going on a month and we are in the same

position they have worked hard how will you get out of it you poor
dears let's hope that it will end one day and that we'll be able to be far
away, very far away from all these brutes goodbye see you soon my
affectionate greetings to the good Zoé and to the naughty little dog
my kind remembrances to the Villa Grisi a kind soldier is taking my
letter to the post with all my heart your

L. GAUTIER*

Mrs Moulton to her mother:

7 May

Never has Paris led such a sober life; there is no noise in the almost
empty and dimly lighted streets; there are no drunkards, and, strange
to say, one hears of no thefts. There are, I believe, one or two small
theatres open, most of the small cafés, and a great many wine-shops.
The soldiers slink about, looking ashamed of their shabby uniforms
and ragged appearance.

Thiers has done all in his power to conciliate the different parties,
but has now concluded that Paris must be conquered by the troops of
Versailles. Every day there comes more disturbing news. How will it
all end? When shall we get out of this muddle? *En attendant*, we live
in a continual fright . . .†

9 May

While we were at breakfast this morning the servant came rushing in,
pale and trembling, and announced to us that pillage had commenced
in the Boulevard Haussmann, just around the corner, and that the
mob was coming toward our house. We flew to the window, and, sure
enough, there we saw a mass of soldiers collected on the other side
of the street, in front of the Princess Mathilde's palace, gesticulating
and pointing over at us . . .

The mob crossed the street, howling and screaming, and on finding
the gate locked began to shake it. The frightened *concierge*, already
barricaded in the lodge, took care not to show himself, which infuri-
ated the riotous crowd to such an extent that they yelled at the top
of their lungs to have the gate opened.

Mr Moulton sent a scared servant to order the still invisible *concierge* to open not only one gate, but all three. He obeyed, trembling and quaking with fear. The Communists [*sic*] rushed into the court-yard, and were about to seize the unhappy *concierge*, when Mr Moulton, seeing that no one else had the courage to come forward, went himself, like the true American he is, . . . out on to the *perron*, and I went with him. His first words (in pure Anglo-Saxon), 'Qu'est-ce que vous voolly ?' made the assembled crowd giggle.

The leader pushed forward, and, presenting a paper with the official seal of the *Comité de Transport*, demanded, in the name of the Commune (*requisitioned*, they call it), everything we had in the way of animals . . .

It was heart-rending to see poor Louis's grief when he led out the dear, gentle horse we loved so fondly; the tears rolled down his cheeks, as they did down mine, and I think a great many of the ruffians around us had a tear of sympathy for our sorrow, for the merriment of a few moments before faded suddenly from their pale and haggard faces . . .

The now subdued mob left us, filing out quietly through the gates; they had come in like roaring lions, but went out like the meekest of lambs.*

On 10 May the Treaty of Frankfurt was signed, and the Franco-Prussian War was officially over. That evening the Palace of the Tuileries was thrown open to the public.

Mr Washburne:

Ten thousand people filled all the apartments, wandering everywhere at their ease, and examining into every nook and corner of the vast palace . . . Great interest centred in the private apartments of the Empress. The gorgeous belongings were everywhere commented upon by the mob. The bath-room of the Empress attracted great attention. It was represented as very handsome, and as a marvel of luxury, beauty and taste. It was surrounded by heavy plate mirrors. The tub was cut out of solid marble. The ceilings were all covered with rich blue silk velvet [*sic*]. The faucets in the bath were of solid silver. All that was seen was described by the Communards as evidence of the profligacy and luxury of the Court, which accounted for the oppression of the people, and for the vast increase of the taxes levied upon them. Not one man in the crowd, it is safe to say, had ever paid a cent of taxes in his life.*

Lili Gautier to her brother:

> *Neuilly,*
> *14 May*
>
> My dear Théo ... I am taking care not to catch any shells so as to keep my skin I hope to see you soon and I always love you
>
> My fondest love
>
> L.G.†

Many innocent Parisians had died, and countless buildings in Paris had been destroyed. The mindless destruction was not over yet, for there still remained the symbols of the imperial past. As early as September Gustave Courbet, the Realist painter and revolutionary, had urged Trochu to demolish the Colonne Vendôme. Contractors had now made a bevel-cut at the base of the Column, to fell it like some gigantic tree; and the demolition, on 16 May, was to be the grandest festivity since the proclamation of the Commune at the end of March. No doubt the Commune hoped that the spectacle would distract Parisians from grim reality: from the besieging army which was drawing ever closer to the city.

Mrs Moulton to her mother:

> *16 May*
>
> The Column Vendôme fell today; they have been working some days to undermine it at the base of the socle. Everyone thought it would make a tremendous crash, but it did not; it fell just where they intended it to fall, toward the rue de la Paix, on some faggots placed to receive it. They were a long time pulling at it; three or four pulleys, and as many ropes, and twenty men tugging with all their might –

et voilà. The figure that replaced the Little Corporal (which is safe somewhere in Neuilly) came to earth in a cloud of dust, and the famous column lay broken in three huge pieces.*

Catulle Mendès:

It was five o'clock in the evening. It had been a beautiful day, and the sun enveloped the Caesar, still erect on the glorious pedestal made of all his victories. The crowd was massed from the two barricades in the rue de la Paix and the rue Castiglione, and it spread as far as the Tuileries and the new Opéra; there were twenty or twenty-five thousand eager spectators. People were talking to each other, accosting perfect strangers, and calling one another citizen . . .

The thing was late in happening, however. The big square was almost empty; there were three hundred people at most, all privileged people with tickets, or wearing masonic sashes, or belonging to some headquarters or other. Bergeret, at a window, was nonchalantly flicking the ash off his cigarette with his little finger; the bands were waiting, massed at the four corners of the square; women were correcting the focus of their lorgnettes, and laughing gaily, in the embrasures of the windows of the Ministère de la Justice. The sentries were restless and fidgeting; the piles of rifles were gleaming; children were yawning along the pavements. The ceremony was late: a test rope had broken. Round the heap of faggots where the statue was to lie were planted flags the colour of revenge . . .

At half-past five there were movements round the barricade in the rue Castiglione. The red sashes of the members of the Commune appeared. There was utter silence.

A moment later the ropes attached to the windlass were tightened. The ropes which came down from the top of the Colonne Vendôme grew taut; the gap in the masonry which had been hollowed out at the base gradually closed up; the statue leant over in the rays of the setting sun, then, suddenly, came through the air in a gigantic salute and fell between the flags with a dull and mighty crash, in the middle of a blinding cloud of dust.†

Ernest A. Vizetelly:

As the dust cleared away, I perceived Glais-Bizoin, one of Gambetta's coadjutors during the war in the provinces, standing on the column's pedestal, waving his hat, with a queer smile upon his punchinello face. Near him stood 'General' Bergeret and several Guards, waving large red flags. Loud were the shouts of 'Vive la Commune!' Right quickly did one of the Guard's bands strike up the 'Marseillaise', but amidst and above it I suddenly heard the strains of 'Hail Columbia!' played violently on a piano by some Yankee girl belonging to a party of Americans who had installed themselves on the first floor of the Hôtel Mirabeau. They came out on to the balcony and were loud in their plaudits . . .

I was forgetting to mention that, before the column fell, an American paid no less than £80 for the privilege of ascending it. He wished to be the last person to do so.*

Catulle Mendès:

And now people wanted pieces, and relics. It was like the time of the 'mementoes of the siege', when they sold little pieces of black bread framed, and under glass. The scramble for gain was going to begin; but the Gardes Nationaux crossed bayonets over the barricades. No one got by. And the crowd soon scattered and went to dinner. 'It's fallen!' they said to new arrivals. 'The statue is decapitated! Nobody was killed!' Street arabs cried out: 'It was bloody good!' Most of the crowd were silent.

Then there was a magnetic effect, when night fell; it seemed that something round you was missing – even to those who still didn't know about the great murder.†

Lili Gautier to her sister Zoé:

Neuilly,
19 May
Dear sister they give us hope that this horrible war will soon be over and the days pass and in the morning the cannon boom the shells

burst at the bottom of the garden Myrza [the cat] growls every time that one passes because it disturbs his dream and the good Théo what has become of him in all this, . . . really mankind is mad how could they create such havoc in such a lovely countryside? The roses are more beautiful than ever the spring is fine, it isn't much fun to have to stay in a cellar like a bottle of vintage wine; you must have seen Monsieur Robelin he should be in Versailles where he was to stay a day or two then go to Nevers he must have told you about the collapse at Neuilly but fortunately hardly any dead take as much care of yourselves as possible, and don't worry about me *at all*, I'm guarding myself like a precious stone for you . . . Estelle, Carlotta, what must they think of all this mix-up but we are alive and that's what matters goodbye and see you soon I hope give a hearty kiss to the dear good Théophile for me think of me as I think of you a black cat has just settled on my paper I embrace you with all my heart.

> Your sister
>
> L.*

Théophile Gautier to his daughter:

> *3, avenue de Saint-Cloud,*
> *Versailles,*
> *20 May 1871*

My dear little girl,

 . . . The end is approaching for us, the entry into Paris cannot be delayed, and in two or three days we'll be able to go and rescue poor Lili from her cellar and see what remains of our house at Neuilly. There was a fire (started by a shell), but Lili bravely put it out with water from the reservoir, otherwise everything would have been burned. The shell had burst in my sister's bed. The kitchen and dining-room have been pock-marked by bullets. There's no damage in your room or mine. Just a few bullets in the studio ceiling. At least this was so a fortnight ago, when I last had news. A brief note from Lili on 15 May proves that she is still alive and awaiting her deliverance with heroic courage. There's nothing in her letter except information about her health. They've pulled down the Vendôme Column, razed and pillaged Thiers' house, they're going to take a hammer to the Sainte Chapelle (monumental fanaticism) and violate the Emperor's tomb, they're going to bury his remains at Clamart in the cemetery of the tortured beside the carcass of Troppmann. To crown the little celebration they will shoot the archbishop and the hostages. It's charming and highly civilised! Unfortunately these aren't reactionaries' inventions to discredit the Republic. They are happening in broad daylight, in the heart of Paris, in front of a population whose soul seems to have vanished, made brutish as it is by this stupid Terror . . . What degradation! Once upon a time twenty-five policemen would have been enough to stuff these scoundrels or rather these drunk gorillas into a lock-up. Now it takes an army . . . I am going to seek some peaceful corner of the earth where I can earn my daily bread and that of my family among rational beings . . .

Your father,
THÉOPHILE GAUTIER*

Next day, 21 May, near the Point-du-Jour, through an undefended gate, the Versailles troops began to pour into the capital.

The destruction of the Vendôme Column

The burning of the rue Royale

Part Five

La Semaine
sanglante

Edward Malet, second secretary at the British Embassy:

22 May

On the eventful morning of Monday, 22 May, I awoke, as usual, but the accustomed sound of the bombardment no longer greeted my ear – another noise replaced it. I sat up in bed and listened. Quick, sharp cracks, incessant, innumerable. Small arms had replaced the cannon; the full significance of the change came home to me at once. I knew that the Versaillais troops were in the Champs-Élysées, and on going to the window I saw the tricolour flag floating over the Arc de Triomphe . . .

We went out into the street, and a singular sight met our eyes. The Communists were rolling barrels down it as fast as they could run. Within an hour they had made two first-rate barricades athwart the Faubourg Saint-Honoré – one at the Élysée, the other at the rue d'Anjou Saint-Honoré. It seemed to be time to close the great gates of the Embassy. At nine o'clock a fusillade began up and down the street.*

Mr Washburne:

It was six o'clock on Monday morning, 22 May, when a friend came to my room and awakened me to tell me that the government troops were in the city, and that the tricolour was floating on the Arc de Triomphe. I dressed hurriedly, and went out to see for myself, as this great monument was but a short distance from where I was staying. When I beheld that proud ensign of France floating in the breeze I felt that Paris was saved, and that a terrible burden had been lifted from my shoulders . . .

Late in the afternoon of Monday, 22 May, Marshal MacMahon, who had command of all the government forces, entered Paris and established his headquarters at Passy. In the evening I rode out to see him to advise him of what I knew in relation to Archbishop Darboy, and to express the hope that the government troops might yet be enabled to save him. The interview was anything but reassuring to me, and I left the headquarters of the marshal feeling that the fate of the Archbishop was sealed.*

Monseigneur Darboy, the Archbishop of Paris, was being held as hostage, with other priests, including the Abbé Deguerry, the curé of the Madeleine. As the Commune grew more desperate, they became more ruthless and vindictive. Raoul Rigault had now given the order that all the hostages were to be shot. They had been held at the prison of Mazas. On the evening of the 22nd, 'the victims – forty of them – the good Darboy, Deguerry, Bonjean, and others – were piled into a transport-wagon with only a board placed across, where they could sit,' and they were taken to La Roquette.†

Paris itself was to suffer a worse fate than any of its inhabitants had imagined. As Marshal MacMahon later recorded:

Since the end of April, the petroleum and all the engines of destruction had been requisitioned. On 23 May, the specially organized companies of fire-lighters, bands of hideous women and Gardes nationaux, drunk, carrying carboys of petroleum, buckets, pumps, gunpowder, had been divided among the different quartiers. At the approach of the troops, and after the pillage of the houses and public establishments, the petroleum was spread over the rooms and staircases; they daubed the walls with it. In an instant the buildings were ablaze from roof to ground . . .
It was no longer vengeance, it was madness.‡

Jules Favre:

23 May

At five o'clock in the morning, I was woken by a messenger from M. Thiers who summoned me to the Presidential lodgings. I found him indescribably moved. 'Look, read this,' he said to me, and handed me a despatch. I was stupefied to see that during the night fires had been lit at the palaces of the Tuileries, the quai d'Orsay and the

Légion-d'honneur; they had fears for the Louvre. A few hours later they informed us that the Palais-Royal and the Hôtel de Ville were in flames. In the meanwhile our soldiers were advancing only slowly, hindered at every step by barricades which they had to outflank by making their way through the houses. The barricade in the place de la Concorde was formidably high, protected by a deep trench, bristling with guns. General Douay captured it, in spite of the desperate efforts of its defenders; then he rushed to the buildings which were on fire and saved the precious collections in our museums by making a large opening in the building. But the library of the Louvre was already nothing but a heap of ashes; science and art lost inimitable treasures. The Bibliothèque Mazarine was about to suffer the same fate, the kegs of petroleum were already accumulated, when the sudden entrance of our valiant sailors set to flight the rascals who were ready to complete their work of destruction. The Préfecture de Police, the Palais de Justice, several rooms in the Gobelins, the buildings of the public storehouse were all in turn a prey to the flames. Wretches, among them, one is ashamed to say, several women and children, were pouring petroleum through the vents in the cellars and then throwing burning matches in . . .*

Ernest A. Vizetelly:

The Rev. R. Ussher of Westbury, who had come into the city with Howard Russell, Lord Ronald Gower, and Mr Trench of the British Legation at Brussels – they stayed at the Hôtel des Quatre Saisons – tells me that he was particularly struck by the awful expressions which he noticed on the faces of the women of the Commune. It was, indeed, for the most part something unnatural, a compound of savagery, revengefulness, despair and ecstatic fervour. It was difficult to surmise, says Mr Ussher, what those women's previous callings had been. I agree with him, and many of the women themselves might have been at a loss to state their former vocations. They had forgotten them. These unfortunate creatures were the outcome of the Franco-German war, of the grim, dark, cold, hungry days of the first siege, of the cruel want, the enforced idleness, the continuous unrest of ten long woeful months. They had suffered more, often far more, than the men had suffered. Even during the Commune they had remained half-starved; they had lost husbands killed in the fighting, children who had wasted away in thousands; despair, rancour and hatred had mastered them; some had taken to drink, some, no doubt, had been women of evil lives, but others had once been happy wives and mothers, careful and painstaking *ménagères*. Many of them were now sheer furies, but it was war, with all its horrors, its losses, its privations, its blood-thirstiness, which had made them such . . .

The very first conflagrations were those ignited in the rue Royale at the corner of the faubourg Saint-Honoré, and they were undoubt-edly designed for the purpose of checking the advance of the soldiers either by way of the boulevards or the rue Saint-Honoré. It was at about four o'clock on Tuesday, 23 May, when some flames suddenly leapt out of the corner-house where Aurelly's *magasin-de-modes* was located. The next house, where there was either a book-shop or a publisher's store-place on the ground floor, was soon in flames, which before long spread to the old English restaurant known as 'His Lord-ship's Larder' . . . Weber, the landlord, and his family had taken refuge in the cellars, and there they perished from suffocation. Sev-eral people also lost their lives in ten other houses which were des-troyed by fire on this point, some of them being in the faubourg Saint-Honoré, whilst others stretched towards the Madeleine. Yet another house was gutted on the other side of the rue Royale, on the corner of the rue Saint Honoré. Mme Decamps, widow of the famous French painter of that name, resided there, and a fine collection of her husband's works was destroyed by the flames.*

Edwin Child:

Got off my sofa about ½ past 7, fire was still raging; about ½ past 9 we began to hear the roaring of the cannon, the gnashing [?] of the mitrailleuses and the continual roar of the fusillade which towards the afternoon became terrible, at the same time the bombs whistled overhead, spreading terror in the whole neighbourhood, those living on the 4th and 5th floors not daring to sleep in their rooms, we also began to perceive fires that appeared to burn from all parts of the city, amongst others the Hôtel de Ville, the Palais de Justice and what appeared the Tuileries but this seems incredible; the cannons fired from the R Rambuteau shook the whole of the pâté of houses and in many, every window was smashed, from stragglers we heard that the troops were gaining ground.

Lovely summer's day.*

Edward Malet:

At five o'clock I was awakened by a servant who said that an officer wanted to see me.

I shuffled on my clothes, and going into the hall found a colonel of the regular army who told me that he desired to examine the position of the barricade at the Rue d'Anjou. I told him that if he did so it would at once attract the fire straight on to the Embassy, which I was there to protect as far as lay in my power, that there were houses to the right and the left of it from whence he could obtain equally good views, and that I could not give him the permission he required.

He said he had spoken to me as a matter of courtesy, and that he required no permission, his orders being to make use of any house, be it an embassy or another, that might serve his purpose, and on that he left me. I went into the drawing-rooms looking out on to the Champs-Élysées, and found the Embassy gardens full of troops. They had made a hole in the wall from Baron Rothschild's garden, which adjoins ours, and were engaged in making another through the wall which separated the garden of the Embassy on the other side from that of Monsieur Péreire. I remained much interested in watching their proceedings, when the colonel again came to me, and told me that he had . . . a request to make to me, which was that I should arrange the dining-room as an ambulance to which his wounded soldiers could be brought. To this I at once assented. I had the long dining-table laid out its full length and mattresses placed upon it, and said to myself, 'It will be a grim remembrance when all this is over and we have our next State dinner'. However, no wounded were brought, and the spectres of dying men do not haunt that hospitable board; but, alas! the colonel was carried back dead through the garden in the afternoon . . .

In the evening we dined in the cellar, and I do not think there was ever a quainter dinner to look at. The roof was vaulted, the walls were of stone. Against these were piled the innumerable articles which we had hastily brought down to save them in case of the Embassy catching fire – piles of archives, precious pieces of furniture, valuables, ciselé clocks and candelabra, china vases, red despatch boxes, all atop of one another . . . In the centre, in vivid contrast of neatness with disorder, was the table laid for dinner with its white tablecloth and silver candlesticks, and, to crown incongruities, Frank Lascelles and myself in evening dress and white ties, waited on by the stately butler and Embassy servants.*

Maxime du Camp:

Night had come, for there were many apartments at the Tuileries, and each of them had had to be given its provision of petroleum and gunpowder. This had taken more than four hours. The plan was very simple: to set fire to the corner wings and the galleries, and as the fire spread it would reach the Salle des Maréchaux, which would explode and bring down the whole palace. Some fifteen men, armed with long rods with lights shining on the end, were seen to pass across the windows, going from the pavillon de Flore towards the pavillon de l'Horloge. In the direction of the pavillon Marsan, a guard who was on his rounds in the basement caught sight of Étienne Boudin and his orderly, the one-armed Albert Sech, crouching near a heap of straw and old papers, each of them with a candle in his hand. The expression on the faces of the incendiaries was so terrible, that the poor man was seized with fright, and fled.†

By ten o'clock that night all was ready. The incendiaries retired to the Louvre barracks; and, as Vizetelly recorded:

The burn

the Tuileries

The whole company sat down to supper, ate and drank copiously, and after partaking of *café noir* at the conclusion of their repast, went out on to the Louvre terrace in order to feast their eyes on the spectacle of the blazing palace. The flames seemed to travel from either end of the great façade – over 1200 feet in length – towards the central cupola-crowned pavilion where Bénot, with artistic feeling, had designedly placed most of his explosives and combustibles. At about 2 o'clock in the morning there came a terrific thunderous shock and uproar, and the whole of the surrounding district trembled. Flames now leapt skyward from the central pavilion of the palace, whose cupola was tossed into the air, whence it fell in blazing fragments, whilst a myriad of sparks rose, rained, or rushed hither and thither, imparting to the awful spectacle much the aspect of a 'bouquet' of fireworks.

Taking a pencil, Bergeret wrote on a slip of paper: 'The last vestiges of Royalty have just disappeared. I wish that the same may befall all the public buildings of Paris.' He handed this note to a young insurgent named Victor Thomas – curiously enough a nephew of General Clément Thomas – and it was taken to the Committee of Public Safety, which was still installed at the Hôtel-de-Ville. Bénot, who had been the principal artisan of the destruction of the Tuileries, was not content with that exploit, for he also helped to set fire to the Louvre library, which comprised over 40,000 volumes, including some very valuable and splendidly bound works.*

Mr Washburne:

24 May

At one o'clock on the morning of 24 May I was awakened by a friend who told me that the Tuileries were all in flames. I immediately hurried to my legation, and sought a position on the roof which gave me a complete view of the fire. It was a starlight night, calm and beautiful. An insurgent battery which had been shelling our part of the city was still sending its bombs into the immediate neighbourhood of our legation every fifteen minutes. The roar of other cannon, the *crépitement* of the mitrailleuses and the sharp rattling of the chassepots, fell upon the stillness of the night. The lurid flames rising over the burning city lighted up half the heavens, and a more terrible scene was hardly ever witnessed.*

Maxime du Camp:

At a quarter past one in the morning, the dome of the Salle des Maréchaux was blown off by the explosion of the powder kegs. It burst, and threw out a whirlwind of sparks, hurled doors and iron-work and joists far and wide, and collapsed in the flames. The spectators marvelled, applauded, and cried: 'Vive la Commune!'†

Edwin Child:

Slept well in spite of the deafening row, but did not undress, could still see the flames from Hôtel de Ville, etc. It seemed literally as if the whole town was on fire, and as if all the powers of hell were let loose upon the town, all day we could hear that terrible din that never ceased for an instant not knowing at what moment our own turn might arrive. Did not dare sleep upstairs bombs having fallen upon nearly every house in the voisinage, fortunately part of the maison was occupied by a dealer in skins who kindly offered us asile (10 women 5 men) slept upon bearskins almost as well as in my bed, much to the astonishment of the others who could not close their eyes for the sinister whistling of the bombs.
    Lovely day.‡

Édouard Thierry:

Eight o'clock. The fires never stop blazing up . . .
    We see the shells passing over the Seine and falling in the place du Châtelet, between the two theatres.
    It seems too probable that the Tuileries is on fire! So long as the Musée du Louvre . . . So long as our beautiful Théâtre-Français . . .
    Another fire breaks out. I'm afraid it may be the fire at the Hôtel de Ville. A Garde national shouts at us, imperiously: 'Shut the

windows! Open the shutters! Shut the windows!' The smoke seems to be coming out in clouds from the clock-tower of the Hôtel de Ville ...

One o'clock. A terrible explosion. All the windows are shaken. A huge column of smoke rises up to the right of the Panthéon. One wonders if this is the barrack-hospital in the Luxembourg – or the Luxembourg itself – which is in flames ...*

Le Bien Public:

The Library of the Louvre was burnt on the night of Tuesday to Wednesday by a band of rascally soldiers of the Commune.

They went into the concierge's room, and threatened him, and ordered him to spread petroleum himself round the precious repository entrusted to his care, unless he preferred to be shot at once. 'Shoot me, but I shan't set fire to the library!' he answered; and his wife, who was present, showed the same firmness and courage. The bandits then deliberated, reached an agreement, and shut these two unfortunate people up in their room, and told them: 'You won't be shot, but you'll both be roasted!' Ten minutes later, the rich and priceless library of the Louvre was in flames; and only by a sort of miracle did its two faithful guardians manage to escape.†

Edmund Ollier:

The escape of Notre-Dame was very remarkable. It is related that, at 3 o'clock on 24 May, M. Hanot, the house-surgeon on duty in the waiting-room of the neighbouring hospital, the Hôtel Dieu, was aroused by a great noise. Casks were being rolled through an opening in an adjacent barricade, and a lieutenant of the National Guards was demanding to be furnished with gimlets, locksmiths' tools, and a candle, in order that he might fire the cathedral. The director of the Hôtel Dieu, however, obtained a respite, on the ground that there were nine hundred sick and wounded in the hospital, and that the destruction of the one building would involve that of the other. Nevertheless, at about eleven o'clock the same morning, fire and smoke were seen issuing from one of the windows of the cathedral. The six house-surgeons were refused the use of the fire-engine; but with the aid of a fireman, and of a number of women and children, they were enabled to quench the flames. A subsequent examination showed that elaborate preparations had been made for consuming this grand old monument of the Middle Ages; but they happily failed. A guard was then organized for preserving the cathedral from further incendiary attempts, and at night that part of the city was in the hands of the Government army.*

Ernest A. Vizetelly:

I was with my father and my brother . . . on the Place de la Concorde, when the whole front of the arcaded Ministry of Finances fell forward into the rue de Rivoli. At that moment my father and brother were actually in front of the ministry, and had to run in desperate haste in order to escape being crushed to death by some of the descending masonry. It came down with a loud crash, and immediately afterwards the atmosphere was darkened by an immense cloud of smoke, in the midst of which were thousands of more or less charred papers, some of which the breeze carried as far as the Place des Invalides, whilst others rained down upon the Place de la Concorde and the Tuileries gardens. We picked up a few of those papers, and among them, I remember, was a petition addressed in 1814 to Louis XVIII, by some nobleman who had returned from exile, and who begged the king either to restore to him his ancestral estates, confiscated during the Revolution, or to grant him a suitable indemnity.†

Marie Colombier, actress and courtesan:

As dusk fell, during the days of exile, we used to gather on the terrace at Saint-Germain, which looked over Paris; it appeared in the distance like the promised land. One evening, we saw a light appearing, and gradually growing; it spread out into jets of fire, stretched out in reddening sheets, and filled the whole of the horizon, the sinister dawn of a conflagration. We looked at each other, and suddenly we understood: 'My God! Those madmen have just set fire to Paris!' It was in fact the Commune which was hoisting its red banner over the capital.

The fire rumbled like a continuous bass, punctuated at intervals by dry crackling sounds. The light became so bright that it lit up the whole terrace: a fearful apotheosis. This scene of horror was bathed in the bloody splendour of the pyres lit by the revolutionary Neros, as if it were in a halo of Bengal lights. After eighteen hundred years, a crime as terrible, as fearfully radiant as the sack of Rome, blazed out under the starry calm of heaven: Paris was burning.

Sparks, borne by the wind, whirled overhead: they were the documents from the Cour des Comptes. Or, rather, they were the history of the Second Empire which was passing, page by page, in the smoke and flames. It was over, this Balzacian dream which had been realised in the romantic adventure of the time ... The great ladies who were really the d'Espards and the Maufrigneuses dreamed of by the creator of the *Comédie humaine;* the elegant careerists who incarnated Rubempré and Rastignac; the creatures of luxury and joy who had all the beauty of Esther, all the wit of Jenny Cadine, had only, now, to grow old and to die. Their reign was over for ever and ever; the ass's skin was worn out, all the goblets at the orgy had been drained. The quadrille from *Orphée aux Enfers* no longer made the brass roar under the chandeliers of the Opéra; there was nothing, now, but the saraband of the *pétroleuses* round the ruins.*

On 24 May, at La Roquette, where the archbishop and others were imprisoned, another dastardly deed was performed. Marshal Mac-Mahon later reported:

Between half-past seven and eight o'clock in the evening, the grille opened; there was a sound of footsteps and the clatter of arms; a band of federates came forward, preceded by an individual with a red sash; some very young men, a few old, drunk, disgusting creatures, peculiar to these wretched days, a fireman, some Gardes nationaux, some volunteers dressed in grey and wearing Garibaldian hats. The summons was made in the midst of the jeers and insults of this company, the victims went downstairs and along the round way, among the Gardes nationaux; they answered the violence only with silence or with calm and noble words . . .

They were: Monseigneur Darboy, Président Bonjean, the Abbé Deguerry, Père Clerc, the Abbé Allard, Père Ducoudray.

When they reached the scene of the crime, G. Ranvier demanded silence. 'This must end,' he said. An officer ordered the hostages to go forward; then Ranvier gave the signal, and there followed a prolonged fire from the firing squad, followed by a few isolated shots. Monseigneur Darboy was the last to remain standing, and he was finished off . . .

After midnight, the chief warder, Ramain, a few federates, Captain Verig and J. Clément came quietly, by the light of a lantern, to search the corpses; one of them hurt himself trying to tear off the Prelate's silver buckle. He then kicked the victim, insulted him, and blasphemed. The bodies were then taken on a hand-cart to Père-Lachaise. Then came the pillage of the few small things left in the cellars. These were shared by François (the Governor of La Roquette), his mistress, and his henchmen.*

Edwin Child:

25 May

Raised myself about 7, could still see smoke arising from everywhere and the reports of the guns became nearer and nearer till about the middle of the day we perceived a few of the *real* troops cautiously moving about and at last near ½ past 4 we were free, with what pleasure we once more walked out, and how freely we breathed, I immediately went off to see if the magasin was burnt, but had not got far before I was stopped to work at the pumps, and what a sight met my eyes destruction everywhere, from the Châtelet to the Hôtel de Ville, all was destroyed, not a room left, worked about ½ an hour then proceeded on my way, saw 3 waggons of dead Communists taken out of ONE yard, crossed Bould Sébastopol, les Halles, R. Neuve St Augustin & on arriving R. Scribe found everything safe then tried to get to my room but found Rue Royale in ruins & conclude my room to be amongst them, then walked to Tuileries & found it but too true all was literally 'gutted' could hardly repress a tear to think that such demons could exist to fire such a monument of works of art.

Lovely day.*

Mrs Moulton to her mother:

The Arc de Triomphe and the Champ de Mars were captured today, and the fighting in the streets has commenced. They are fighting like mad in the Faubourg St Honoré. When I open the door of the vestibule I can hear the yelling and screaming of the rushing mob; it is dreadful, the spluttering of the fusillades and the guns overpower all other noises. We hope deliverance is at hand; but who knows how long before we have peace and quiet again?†

Jules Pau:

One of the most impressive barricades, as far as the defence was concerned, was the one in the rue Royale. Equipped with cannon and mitrailleuses, it bombarded the place de la Concorde without respite. In order to make themselves masters of it, the soldiers went down the rue Boissy-d'Anglais and crossed the gardens which go along this street and the ones attached to the rue du Faubourg Saint-Honoré; they were supported by other troops coming from the boulevard Haussmann, the boulevard Malesherbes and the rue Tronchet. The insurgents were obliged to abandon the barricade, but they could not escape, for their escape-route was cut off. They tried to take refuge in the Madeleine.

The soldiers followed them there, and, forcing the doors which the federates attempted to barricade, they burst into the church and attacked without mercy, everyone who was there.

None of the three hundred insurgents who were cut off in this building came out alive.‡

Lord Lyons to Lord Granville:

Versailles, 26 May 1871

The state of Paris is heartbreaking. The night I spent there (24th) was calculated to give one an idea of the infernal regions. Fires in all directions, the air oppressive with smoke and unpleasant odours, the incessant roar of cannon and musketry and all kinds of strange sounds. For the forty-eight hours before my arrival, the members of the Embassy and all in the house were in imminent danger; a fire raging in the next street but one, shells falling on the roof which might set fire to the house at any moment, and shot flying so fast on both sides that escape in case of fire would have been hardly possible. It is a great satisfaction to me that every one in the house behaved well. Of the members of the Embassy I was quite sure, and all the men servants appeared to have shown pluck and alacrity in rushing to the places where the shells fell, in order to extinguish the fire in case of need. Malet [sometime Sir Edward Malet, H.M. Ambassador to Berlin] has a first-rate head, and directed everything with his usual coolness and self-possession.

One bit of a shell is said to have fallen in the garden yesterday morning, but it certainly did no mischief, and there was no appearance of danger while I was there. I cannot, however, feel quite comfortable so long as the insurgents hold the Buttes de Chaumont. They must, I should hope, be on the point of being driven out at the moment I write. Little or no intelligence of what was going on in the town could be obtained. The least inconvenience on leaving one's house was to be seized upon to form a chain to hand buckets. Sentries stopped our progress in almost every direction; arrests were frequent and summary executions the order of the day.*

Le Bien Public:

27 May

The members of the Commune had mined the sewers from the Hôtel de Ville to the Banque [de France]. They intended to blow up the whole of this quartier.

They had therefore concealed prodigious quantities of chemical products in these underground pipes. No doubt they did not have the time to put this abominable plan into action.

Yesterday evening, some soldiers from the engineers, sent on reconnaissance into these sewers, found *fifteen people*, posted by the incendiaries, asphyxiated by the emanations of the products which they had prepared.

More than a thousand telegraph wires have been cut in the sewers; they were intended to carry the fire to the four quarters of Paris. The Louvre and the Invalides escaped by miracle.

In the Luxembourg quartier a number of women and children have been shot for firing on the soldiers.

At six o'clock in the evening, near the new Opéra, a woman shot a senior infantry officer with a revolver, and killed him. She was immediately shot.*

The violence was still hideous. Yet Ludovic Halévy, who came that day from Versailles to Paris, was amazed, already, by the signs of returning life.

In the midst of these mines and fires, while they were still fighting on the heights of Père-Lachaise, what certainly struck me most was the immediate resumption of life in this great human ant-hill. Behind the victorious troops from Versailles, life suddenly sprang up again between the paving-stones . . .

In the last ten months, I have seen many extraordinary things, but nothing stranger, nothing more fantastic than what I saw there, a little while ago, with my own eyes . . . Between the pont Royal and the pont de la Concorde, some anglers – there were twelve of them, I counted – had settled down quite peacefully, and were not in the least concerned with what was happening above their heads. Their eyes were fixed on the little corks which were bobbing about on the end of their lines, and they were taking advantage of all these disorders *to fish at a prohibited time.**

28 May

RÉPUBLIQUE FRANÇAISE

Inhabitants of Paris,

The French Army has come to save you. Paris is liberated. At four o'clock, our soldiers took the last positions occupied by the insurgents.

General headquarters, 28 May 1871.

Marshal of France, Commander-in-Chief,

de MACMAHON, Duke of Magenta†

Edwin Child:

Up at 8. Church at 11 . . . Had a walk aux Chps. Élysées and round Arc de Triomphe, was glad to find it almost uninjured, although many of the houses round about had suffered severely . . .

At 4 a.m. the last vestiges of the revolution were extinguished, and the whole of the city was in the hands of the troops after 8 full days bloody fighting.‡

Mrs Moulton to her mother:

MacMahon has stormed the barricades and has entered Paris, taking fifty thousand prisoners. Gallifet has ordered thousands to be shot.

We are rescued from more horrors. Thank God! these days of trembling and fear are over . . .

We hear that Auber became quite crazy and wandered out on the ramparts, and was killed with the soldiers. He deserved a better fate, my dear old friend! I am sure his heart was broken . . .

Seventy-two days of Communism have cost France 850,000,000 francs.§

Rev. William Gibson:

What a week since last Sunday! No week during the siege was anything to be compared with it. My heart has been full of anguish. This is Whit-Sunday. Oh that God may bestow on us abundantly the gift of the Holy Spirit! Then I do not despair of the resuscitation of France and of Paris. But men have not been willing to acknowledge the existence of God nor of the Holy Spirit. Hence the abyss of misery into which they have fallen. Madame Sabatier this morning gave us a good *déjeuner*, a roast with carrots. After we had finished she told us that it was a morsel of the horse of an insurgent commandant, which had been killed near her son's house.*

Edmond de Goncourt:

We are walking in smoke; we are breathing in air which smells at the same time of burning and of furniture-polish, and, on every side, we can hear the *pshit* of the pumps. In many places there are still horrible traces and remains of the battle. Here it is a dead horse; there, by the paving-stones in a half-demolished barricade, are some képis bathed in a pool of blood.†

Edwin Child:

Sunday, 28 May 1871

Dear Father,

Here is now arrived the 7th day of this horrible carnage, and still is to be heard the boom of the cannon, the defence being desperate in that birthplace of infection, Belleville, Ménilmontant and Père-Lachaise, the whole cream of the Communists are there united together and make their stand with a courage or rather despair worthy of a better cause, their losses must have been enormous, heaps of dead bodies laying in various parts of the town, I saw 3 large railway vans crammed full of them and all taken out of the same courtyard, behind the Hôtel de Ville I was told there is a street full piled in heaps and it is said that over 500 perished in the flames of the Hôtel de Ville, the demons they can be called by no other name. I had a narrow squeak of it, but then everybody may say the same, on the Monday morning I was woke up [*sic*] by one of my friends hammering at the door and shouting that the troops had entered, in less than 5 minutes I was dressed and tried to get to my room in the Faubg St. Honoré, but

that I found impossible bullets whizzing past like hailstones, I felt
in a fix having no provisions at the shop, after a little thought, I determined to beat a retreat upon an Englishman living in the R. du
Temple & who I knew was prepared for a siege. This was no easy
matter, it being about ½ past 9 & shells falling round the Opéra freely
enough, however by making a circuit and assisting the *fédérés* with
their accursed barricades I arrived safely & jolly glad my friend was
to have a companion, we passed Monday quietly enough card playing
& could hardly hear the cannon at all, the night also passed quietly,
but Tuesday morning, began such a row as to make even a brave man
quake, & it was at this moment that fires began to add to the horrors
of the scene, our house was one of 7 stories & commanded a view of
nearly the whole town, we could see every fire as it began & at one
moment I thought the whole city was doomed, on the Wednesday we
seemed encircled by fires, the shrill whistling of the bombs, the harsh
grating of the mitrailleuses and the continual roar of the gun firing
being something indescribable, this we had to endure till ½ past 4 in
the aft^n of Thursday, when our hearts were gladdened by the sight
of the brave troops of the line, & it was with feelings of thankfulness
that we could gaze upon their smoke blackened faces, the poor fellows
had no sooner finished than they laid down and went to sleep tired
out. I immediately got ready to bolt to the shop to see if all was right,
but had hardly got beyond the immediate neighbourhood, before I
was seized to work at the pumps, and what a sight to see never could
I have believed it, whole streets demolished not a room escaped, and
the pumps were next to useless might as well have used cans of water,
the largest is not the size of those used for chimneys in London, with
12 steam fire engines, half the damage done might have been averted,
and then to see the people trying to escape working the pumps at such
a moment, why in London, hundreds of willing hands would have
been ready, but here everybody tries to shirk what is but a common
duty. I see that London has offered the loan of a few engines, but they
arrive too late, the damage is irretrievable, when I saw the Tuileries
I could hardly help shedding a tear, and the superb building of the

Council of State and heaven knows what besides. The damage is not confined to public edifices, it was quite sufficient that the house was handsome for it to be doomed, the immense clothing establishment of the 'Belle Jardinière', almost a palace, has been burned, a considerable portion of the Boul^d Sebastopol, the Rue de Rivoli upon *both* sides from the Boul^d Sebastopol to the Hôtel de Ville, in fact hardly a street but that has one or more houses burnt, the Rue Royale, that is the street in front of the Madeleine, leading to the Pl. de la Concorde, has the left hand side entirely destroyed from the Faub͟g St Honoré to the Madeleine, you doubtless remember his Lordship's Larder it is now a heap of ruins, Allen's shop escaped by a miracle, of the house next door not even the walls remain, my room was two doors off and is also untouched with the exception of the windows being broken, and the loss of my pail that they took for making a chain, fancy putting out a house of 7 stories on fire, with pails of water and then people have cheek enough to say 'They manage these things better in France.' The Arc de Triomphe has suffered but very little, one of the fountains in the Pl. de la Concorde is smashed and also many of the lamp-posts and one of the large [word illegible] statues but it has not suffered so much as I expected.

There is but little doubt that if the troops had been 48 hours later, the whole town would have been burned to the ground & God knows how many innocent victims would have been destroyed, as it is the blood runs cold with the various accounts we read every day in the papers, in one house in the R. Royale it is said that 30 poor women were burned, all in the pangs of childbirth, 40 of the soldiers were poisoned by women who offered them wine in the Market-place, such devils are not fit to live, shooting is by far too good for them, the women behaved like tigresses, throwing petroleum everywhere & distinguishing themselves by the fury with which they fought, a convoi of nearly four thousand passed the Boulevards this afternoon, such figures you never saw, blackened with powder, all in tatters and filthy dirty, a few with chests exposed to show their sex, the women with their hair dishevelled & of a most ferocious appearance, some

few looked decent but they were few, by the time that they arrive at
Versailles their appearance will not have improved: quantities are
shot every day and I'm now sick of bloodshed and burning houses, it
will require all the energies of the people to restore Paris & to recover
their trade, but if they take the lesson to heart, the price in a few years
may not appear as being too heavy. It would be useless my recapitu-
lating everything, as you see the list of everything destroyed, in the
journals, every street can show something, broken lamp-posts, trees
splintered, windows broken, etc. The troops have behaved splendidly,
they stuck to their work like Britons, & many is the act of bravery that
might be told, & of wonderful escapes. Mr Williams' agent (Shep-
herd) received a shell right in the middle of his plate glass front,
Capts' [sic] shop is uninjured not even a scratch, what a trade glaziers
will do for a wk. or two, & builders for years almost, who is to pay all
this damage with the addition of 200,000,000 for the Prussians I
would rather be Capts' clerk than Chancellor of the Exchequer. What
do the papers say respecting the International now, I would string em
all up the cutthroat vagabonds.

Love to all,
EDWIN

29th. Just received Harriett's & Mother's letters.*

Edmund Ollier:

Acres of smoking ruins – vistas of shattered and blackened columns
belonging to buildings that had once been among the finest in
Europe – roofless palaces, devastated churches, houses utterly destroyed, or dinted with shot and shell – these were the sad sights which
met the eye in Paris, as the results of that Republic which M. Favre
and his friends had been trying for years to establish, and which they
did not know how to manage when they had got it. At one time the
fires seemed so menacing, and so far beyond the power of the Parisian
firemen to subdue, that M. Thiers, on 25 May, asked Lord Lyons, our
inmbassador in France, for the assistance of the London Fire Brigade
A putting out the conflagration. The request was at once telegraphed

to the proper quarter, and Lord Granville authorised an expenditure of £1,000 to send over a body of English firemen; he also set aside a Government vessel for their conveyance. Arrangements were made for despatching twelve engines and a hundred men; but, on the 26th, the French Government telegraphed that a mastery had been obtained over the flames . . . But, although by this time all fear of the fires spreading was at an end, it was still some days before they were extinguished. Passers-by in the streets were forced to assist in pumping on the ruins, and in burying the dead . . . The condition of Père-Lachaise was particularly horrible. As late as 31 May, the dead lay about the grass in a double tier, powdered over with a coating of chloride of lime . . .

Smoke yet rose in heavy volumes from the chief centres of conflagration, and the remains of barricades mixed with heaps of rubbish, still cumbered the streets. But the sightseers were abroad, and it was shocking to see the levity with which the Parisians, of both sexes and of all ages, ate and drank, and laughed and flirted, and made joyous holiday, amidst the ruins of their fallen city. A decree of M. Thiers, dated 29 May, ordered the disarmament of Paris, and the dissolution of the National Guard of the Department of the Seine; and, in a few days, more than 370,000 rifles had been given up or seized. Marshal MacMahon, moreover, required the National Guards to deliver their uniforms, and bluntly said, in an order of the day, that he would have no other uniform than that of the French army visible in the streets of Paris . . . In consequence of these salutary measures, Paris, in the parts that had not been burnt, began to resume its wonted aspect with greater rapidity than might have been expected.*

The postscript was written, years later, by Dr Thomas Evans, the American dentist who had smuggled the Empress Eugénie out of Paris.

For many long years one huge pile of blackened walls, the remains of what was once the Palace of the Tuileries, loomed up in the very centre of the city, solemn, grand, and mysterious, like a funereal

monument, to remind the world of the uncertain life of governments
– in France. It was only in 1883 that, becoming apparently ashamed
of this startling exhibition of the savagery of the mob, of this vestige
of the reign of the Commune in the *Ville Lumière*, the Government
ordered the demolition of these ruins, and covered with fresh turf
and flowers the ground on which had stood the home of the most
famous kings of France. Every trace of the palace has been removed,
effaced or carefully covered up. And here it is, in this new and formal
garden, that to-day the children with their nurses gather together in
hushed silence, and the idlers stop to watch Pol, the bird-charmer,
as he stands on the grass by the laurel bushes while the pigeons hop
about his feet picking up the crumbs he lets fall.*

Notes

INTRODUCTION

13 *Whitehurst: *My Private Diary during the Siege of Paris*, I, 3
†Ibid, 6
‡*The Times*, 5 September 1870
14 *Whitehurst: op. cit., 11, 13, 14, 15
†American Lady, An: *Pictures from Paris . . .*, 91

Part One PREPARATION

17 *O'Shea: *An Iron-bound City*, I, 49–50
18 *Hoffman: *Camp, Court and Siege*, 180
19 *American Lady, An: op. cit., 94–6
†Cabrol: *Paris pendant le siège*, 15 sqq.
20 *O'Shea: op. cit., 8, 9, 40
†Quoted by Horne: *The Fall of Paris*, 50
21 *Claretie: *La Guerre nationale*, 222–3
†Quoted by Whitehurst: op. cit., I, 59
22 *9 September 1870. From a copy in the author's collection.
23 *11 September 1870. From a copy in the author's collection.
†Adam: *Mes illusions et nos souffrances pendant le Siège de Paris*,
61–2
24 *Favre: *Le Gouvernement de la Défense nationale*, I, 401–2
†Adam: op. cit., 67–8
25 *Blumé: *Campaign, 1870–1871*, 19
†15 September 1870. Un Bourgeois de Paris: *Journal du Siège*,
5–6
‡To Charles Ritter. Renan: *Correspondance*, 330, 331
26 *Whitehurst: op. cit., I, 78–9, 88–9
†Goncourt: *Journal*, IX, 45
‡Blumenthal (ed.): *Journals of Field-Marshal Count von
Blumenthal*, 128

27 *Oxford Graduate, An: *Inside Paris during the Siege*, 26, 27
28 *Labouchère: *Diary of the Besieged Resident in Paris*, 1–2
   †Mme Quinet: *Paris. Journal du siège*, 77–8
29 *Vandam: *An Englishman in Paris*, 420–1
   †Mme Quinet: loc. cit.
   ‡Rochefort: *Les Aventures de ma vie*, II, 280
32 *Vandam: op. cit., 422–4, 425–6
   †Heylli, G. d' (ed.): *Journal du Siège de Paris*, I, 173, 174
   ‡Lasalle: *La musique pendant le siège de Paris*, 44–5
   §Edgar Quinet: *Le Siège de Paris . . .* , 13
33 *Claretie: op. cit., 213

Part Two PARIS UNDER SIEGE

37 *Anon: *Diary of the Siege of Paris, taken from* Galignani's Messenger. Foreword.
   †Anon: *Histoire de la Guerre . . .* , 44–5
38 *Blumé: *Campaign, 1870–1871*, 23, 24
   †Anon: *Life in Paris before the War and during the Siege*, 52
39 *Dabot: *Griffonnages quotidiens d'un bourgeois du quartier latin*, 51–2
   †Buckle (ed.): *The Letters of Queen Victoria*, 71
40 *25 September 1870. Ibid, 72, 73
   †Blumenthal (ed.): op. cit., 131–2
45 *Gautier: *Tableaux de Siège*, 63 sqq.
   †Whitehurst: *My Private Diary during the Siege of Paris*, I, 120–1
   ‡Anon: *Life in Paris . . .* , 54
46 *Labouchère: op. cit., 17
   †Heylli, G. d' (ed.): op. cit., I, 214
   ‡Hugo: *Choses vues. 1870–1885*, 89
47 *Oxford Graduate, An: op. cit., 40–1
48 *Labouchère: op. cit., 19
   †Busch: *Bismarck in the Franco-Prussian War*, I, 178
   ‡Hozier: *The Franco-Prussian War*, II, 319

50 *Officier d'État-major, Un: *Le Siège de Paris illustré*, 70–1
   †Bowles: *The Defence of Paris*, 63–4
51 *Goncourt: op. cit., IX, 54
53 *Labouchère: op. cit., 28–9, 31, 34–5
   †Oxford Graduate, An: op. cit., 35–6
54 *Whitehurst: op. cit., I, 158–9
   †Bowles: op. cit., 70–1
   ‡Busch: op. cit., I, 181–2
55 *29 September 1870. Copy in the author's collection.
56 *Dabot: op. cit., 55
57 *Labouchère: op. cit., 62–3
58 *Anon: *Life in Paris* . . . , 57
   †Busch: op. cit., I, 195
   ‡Anon: *Life in Paris* . . . , loc. cit.
   § Goncourt: op. cit., IX, 62–3
59 *Anon: *Life in Paris* . . . , 57
   †Gautier: op. cit., 120–1
60 *Bowles: op. cit , 87
   †Heylli, G d' (ed.): op. cit., II, 9 sqq.
61 *Queen Victoria: op. cit., 73
   †Quoted by Lafosse: op. cit., I, 372
62 *Edwin Child's Diary. King's College, London
   †Officier d'État-major, Un: op. cit., 76
63 *Officier de marine, Un: *Le Siège de Paris*, 22–3
   †Hozier: op. cit., II, 314–15
   ‡Whitehurst: op. cit., I, 209
64 *American Lady, An: op. cit., 201–2
   †23 October 1870. Dabot: op. cit., 72
   ‡Labouchère: op. cit., 208
   § O'Shea: op. cit., I, 151, 152
65 *8 October 1870. Thierry: *La Comédie-Française pendant les deux sièges*, 104
   †Ibid, 99, 100, 101
66 *Gautier, op. cit., 70 and passim

67 *Officier de marine, Un: op. cit., 24
†Daudet: *Lettres à un absent*, 7
‡Mme Quinet: op. cit., 102–3

68 *6 October 1870. Bowles: op. cit., 106
†Hugo: op. cit., 93–4

69 *Officier de marine, Un: op. cit., 25–6

70 *Labouchère: op. cit., 79–80
†Edwin Child's Diary. King's College, London

71 *Boissonnas: *Une Famille pendant la guerre*, 63–4

72 *Labouchère: op. cit., 105–6
†Officier d'État-major, Un: op. cit., 91

73 *Ollier: *History of the War*, I, 381–2

74 *17 March 1871. Fidus: *La Révolution de septembre. La Capitulation. La Commune*, 392–3
†Goncourt: op. cit., IX, 71

75 *15 October 1870. Heylli, G. d' (ed.): op. cit., II, 117–18
†Cabrol: op. cit., 72
‡Busch: op. cit., I, 241

76 *Anon: *Before Paris*, 7–8
†Flaubert: *Correspondance, 1865–1870*, 566

77 *Bowles: op. cit., 95 sqq.

78 *31 October 1870. From a copy in the author's collection.

80 *Anon: *Before Paris*, 11 sqq.
†O'Shea: op. cit., I, 44

81 *Oxford Graduate, An: op. cit., 133 sqq.

86 *Gautier: op. cit., 95 sqq.
†Boissonnas: op. cit., 105

87 *Whitehurst: op. cit., I, 336–7
†Hoffman: op. cit., 209
‡Bowles: op. cit., 195, 196

88 *Anon: *Before Paris*, 23–4

89 *14 November 1870. Copy in the author's collection

90 *Officier de la Marine, Un: op. cit., 76–7
†Whitehurst: op. cit., II, 57, 62

‡Bowles: loc. cit.
§Child Papers. King's College, London.
91 *23 November 1870. Goncourt *Journal*, IX, 118
†Washburne: *Recollections of a Minister to France*, I, 235
‡Ollier: op. cit., I, 353
92 *Got: *Journal*, II, 106–7
†Whitehurst: op. cit., II, 74
93 *30 November 1870. Copy in the author's collection.
94 *Dabot: op. cit., 104
†Anon: *Before Paris*, 41–3
95 *Labouchère: op. cit., 224
†Edwin Child's Diary. King's College, London.
‡Goncourt: op. cit., IX, 130
97 *Gautier: op. cit., 112–16
98 *8 December 1870. Dabot: op. cit., 113
†Adam: op. cit., 266
99 *Hoffman: op. cit., 210–11
†Whitehurst: op. cit., II, 124
‡Mme Quinet: op. cit., 204–5
100 *15 December 1870. Copy in the author's collection.
†Whitehurst: op. cit., II, 131
101 *Labouchère: op. cit., 241–2
†Newton: *Lord Lyons*, I, 348
102 *Whitehurst: op. cit., II, 158
103 *Labouchère: op. cit., 267–8
105 *Gautier: op. cit., 122–5
†Officier de la marine, Un: op. cit., 111–12
106 *Blumenthal: op. cit., 249–50
†Dabot: op. cit., 128
‡Whitehurst: op. cit., II, 172
107 *Mme Quinet: op. cit., 240
†Buckle: op. cit., 101–2, 103
108 *Dabot: op. cit., 133–4
†Whitehurst: op. cit., II, 187

109 *Favre: op. cit., II, 477–9
110 *Vandam: op. cit., 462–3
     †Blumé: op. cit., 240
111 *Favre: op. cit., II, 485
112 *Ibid, II, 486
114 *Labouchère: op. cit., 317–18, 319–21
     †Whitehurst: op. cit., II, 233
     ‡Buckle: op. cit., 111
115 *Moltke: *The Franco-German War of 1870–71*, 363 sqq.
     †Mme Quinet: op. cit., 302
116 *Edwin Child's Diary. King's College, London.
     *Moltke: loc. cit.
117 *Brunon: *Siège de Paris. Journal du Siège du Fort de Vanves*,
     75–6

Part Three *THE TROUBLED PEACE*

121 *Dabot: op. cit., 150
122 *Bourgeois de Paris, Un: op. cit., 880–1
     †Buckle: op. cit., 117
123 *Moltke: loc. cit.
     †Mme Quinet: op. cit., 312
     ‡Whitehurst: op. cit., II, 280–1, 283
124 *Officier de la marine, Un: op. cit., 164
     †Ducrot: *La Vie militaire du Général Ducrot*, II, 459–60
125 *Forbes: *My Experiences of the War between France and Germany*,
     II, 402–3
126 *Hozier: op. cit., II, 315
     †Reid: *Memoirs of Sir Edward Blount*, 212
     ‡Hozier: op. cit., II, 313
127 *Reid: op. cit., 218–19
     †Vizetelly, Ernest A.: *My Adventures in the Commune*, 19–20
128 *Hoffman: op. cit., 239–40
     †Vizetelly: op. cit., 336
     ‡Daudet: op. cit., 8–9

129 *Labouchère: op. cit., 380
   †Blumenthal: op. cit., 307
130 *16 February 1871. Copy in the author's collection.
131 *[February 1871.] Copy in the author's collection.
132 *22 February 1871. Copy in the author's collection.
133 *Anon: *Before Paris*, 91 sqq.
   *Got: op. cit., II, 110
134 *Blumenthal: op. cit., 321–2
   †Whitehurst: op. cit., II, 332, 335
   ‡O'Shea: op. cit., II, 340–1
   § Whitehurst: op. cit., II, 335–6
135 *Busch: op. cit., I, 346
   †Anon: *Diary of the Siege of Paris, taken from* Galignani's
      Messenger, 169 sqq.
   ‡Thierry: op. cit., 328–9
137 *Anon: *Before Paris*, 101 sqq.
   †Thierry: op. cit., 330
138 *Anon: *Before Paris*, loc. cit.
   †Reid: op. cit., 227–8
139 *Newton: op. cit., I, 371–2
140 *2 March 1871. From a copy in the author's collection.
   †Anon: *Diary of the Siege of Paris, taken from* Galignani's
      Messenger, 171–2
   ‡Forbes: op. cit., II, 465
141 *4 March 1871. Flaubert: *Correspondance, 1871–1873*, 41–2
   †5 March 1871. From a copy in the author's collection.
142 *Bouniols: *Thiers au pouvoir . . .* , 34–5

Part Four THE COMMUNE

145 *Child Papers. King's College, London.
146 *Anon: *Paris-Commune. Le Siège Versaillais*, 43
148 *Hegermann-Lindencrone: *In the Courts of Memory*, 270 sqq.
149 *Newton: op. cit., I, 376–7
150 *25 March 1871. Copy in the author's collection.

†Buckle: op. cit., 124, 125
151 *Vizetelly: op. cit., 85–6
†Washburne: op. cit., II, 57
152 *Newton: op. cit., I, 380
†Washburne: op. cit., II, 68–9
153 *Gibson: *Paris during the Commune*, 63
155 *6 April 1871. Copy in the author's collection.
157 *Vizetelly: op. cit., 163–8
†Gibson: op. cit., 73
158 *Fidus: *La Révolution de septembre. La Capitulation – La Commune*, 421, 422
†Hozier: op. cit., 368
‡Heylli, G. d' (ed.): *Journal d'un habitant de Neuilly*, 17–18
160 *Vizetelly: op. cit., 175, 179–80
161 *Child Papers. King's College, London.
162 *Vizetelly: op. cit., 182, 183, 183–4
†Heylli, G. d' (ed.): op. cit., 19
163 *Vizetelly: op. cit., 218–19
†Gibson: *Paris during the Commune, 1871*, 89–90
164 *Ibid, 104–5
165 *19 April 1871. Copy in the author's collection.
†Washburne: op. cit., II, 100
‡Newton: op. cit., I, 382
166 *21 April 1871. Copy in the author's collection.
†Child Papers. King's College, London.
167 *Vizetelly: op. cit., 226–7
168 *29 April 1871. Copy in the author's collection.
169 *6 May 1871. Copy in the author's collection.
†Hegermann-Lindencrone: op. cit., 317, 318
170 *Ibid, 320 sqq.
171 *Washburne: op. cit., II, 136, 137
†14 May 1871. Copy in the author's collection.
172 *Hegermann-Lindencrone: op. cit., 329
†Mendès: *Les 73 journées de la Commune*, 282–5

173 *Vizetelly: op. cit., 281, 283
   †Mendès: loc. cit.
174 *19 May 1871. Copy in the author's collection.
175 *20 May 1871. Copy in the author's collection.

Part Five *LA SEMAINE SANGLANTE*

179 *Malet: *Shifting Scenes*, 318–19
180 *Washburne: op. cit., II, 139, 150
   †Hegermann-Lindencrone: op. cit., 332
   ‡Quoted by Amodru: *La Roquette*, 327–8
181 *Favre: op. cit., III, 445
182 *Vizetelly: op cit., 316–17, 323
183 *Edwin Child's Diary. King's College, London.
184 *Malet: op. cit., 322–4, 325
   †Du Camp: *Les Convulsions de Paris*, II, 204–5
185 *Vizetelly: op. cit., 329–30
186 *Washburne: op. cit., II, 151
   †Du Camp: op. cit., II, 208
   ‡Edwin Child's Diary. King's College, London.
187 *Thierry: op. cit., 465
   †Undated cutting. Child Papers. King's College, London.
188 *Ollier: op. cit., II, 513
   †Vizetelly: op. cit., 334–5
189 *Colombier: *Mémoires. Fin d'Empire*, 318 sqq.
190 *Quoted by Amodru: op. cit., 342–4
191 *Edwin Child's Diary. King's College, London.
   †Hegermann-Lindencrone: op. cit., 334
   ‡Pau: *La Délivrance de Paris*, 18–19
192 *Newton: op. cit., I, 386–7
193 *Le Bien Public*, 27 May 1871. Child Papers. King's College,
   London.
194 *Halévy: *Notes et Souvenirs*, 44–5
   †Pau: op. cit., 15
   ‡Edwin Child's Diary. King's College, London.

§ Hegermann-Lindencrone: op. cit., 334
195 *Gibson: loc. cit.
 †Goncourt: *Journal*, X, 13–14
198 *Child Papers. King's College, London.
199 *Ollier: op. cit., II, 510, 512
200 *Crane (ed.): *The Memoirs of Dr Thomas W. Evans*, II, 588

Select Bibliography

English works are published in London, French works in Paris, unless otherwise stated.

ADAM, Mme Juliette [Juliette Lamber] *Mes illusions et nos souffrances pendant le Siège de Paris.* (Lemerre. 1906)

AMERICAN LADY, An *Pictures from Paris. In War and in Siege.* (Bentley. 1871.)

AMODRU, M. l'Abbé Laurent *La Roquette.* (Lecoffre. 1887.)

ANON. *Diary of the Siege of Paris, taken from* Galignani's Messenger, *the English Paper published in that Capital.* (Simpkin, Marshall. 1871.)

——*Histoire du Siège de Paris. Mémorandum journalier.* (Moronval. 1871.)

——*Histoire de la Guerre de 1870–1871, du Siège de Paris et de la Commune.* (Librairie des villes et des campagnes. 1872.)

——*Before Paris, 1870–1871.* Letters from a Prussian before Paris to the Editor of *The Scotsman.* (Berlin. Francke. 1871.)

——*Life in Paris before the War and during the Siege.* (Diprose & Bateman. 1871.)

——*The War Correspondence of* The Daily News *1870.* (Macmillan. 1871.)

——*Paris-Commune. Le Siège Versaillais.* (Degorce-Cadot. 1871.)

AUDEBRAND, Philippe *Histoire intime de la Révolution du 18 mars. Comité central et commune.* (Dentu. 1871.)

BALDICK, Robert *The Siege of Paris.* (Batsford. 1964.)

BLEIGNERIE, H. de, et DANGIN, E. *Paris incendié, 1871. Album historique.* (Jarry. 1872.)

BLUMÉ, William *Campaign, 1870–1871. The Operations of the German Armies in France, from Sedan to the end of the War. From the journals of the headquarters staff by William Blumé, major in the Prussian Ministry of War.* Translated by E. M. Jones, Major 20th Foot. 2nd. edition. (King. 1872.)

BLUMENTHAL, Count A. von (ed.) *Journals of Field-Marshal Count von Blumenthal for 1866 and 1870–71.* Translated by Major A. D. Gillespie-Anderson. (Arnold. 1903.)

BOISSONNAS, Mme B. *Une Famille pendant la guerre, 1870–1871* (Hetzel. 1873.)

BOUNIOLS, Gaston *Thiers au pouvoir (1871–1873). Texte de ses lettres. Annoté et commenté par Gaston Bouniols.* (Delagrave. 1921.)

BOURGEOIS DE PARIS, Un *Journal du Siège, 1870–1871.* (Dentu. 1872.)

BOURNAND, François *Le clergé pendant la Commune.* (Tolra. 1892.)

BOWLES, Thomas Gibson *The Defence of Paris; Narrated as it was seen by Thomas Gibson Bowles, Special Correspondent of* The Morning Post *in Paris during the Siege.* (Sampson Low. 1871.)

BRUNON, Général *Siège de Paris. Journal du Siège du Fort de Vanves. Par le Général Brunon, ex-Commandant supérieur de ce fort.* (Dentu. 1887.)

BUCKLE, G. E. (ed.) *The Letters of Queen Victoria.* Second series. Vol. II. (Murray. 1926.)

BUSCH, Dr. Moritz *Bismarck in the Franco-German War, 1870–1871.* Authorised translation. 2 vols. (Macmillan. 1879.)

CABROL, Édouard *Paris pendant le siège.* (Bruxelles. Office de publicité. 1871.)

CHAIX, A. *Souvenirs du Siège de Paris*. (Chaix. 1890.)

CLARETIE, Jules *Histoire de la Révolution de 1870–1871*. (Aux bureaux du journal *L'Éclipse*. 1872.)

——*La Guerre nationale, 1870–1871*. (Lemerre. 1871.)

——*Paris assiégé. Tableaux et Souvenirs. Septembre 1870 – Janvier 1871*. (Lemerre. 1871.)

CLARKE, Capt. F. C. H. (tr.) *The Franco-German War, 1870–1871*. Translated from the German Official Account. 2 vols. (H.M.S.O. 1874, 1876.)

COLOMBIER, Marie *Mémoires. Fin d'Empire*. (Flammarion. 1898.)

CRANE, Edward A. (ed.) *The Memoirs of Dr. Thomas W. Evans. Recollections of the Second French Empire*. 2 vols. (Fisher Unwin, 1905.)

DABOT, Henri *Griffonnages quotidiens d'un bourgeois du quartier latin. Du 14 mai 1869 au 2 décembre 1871*. (Péronne. Quentin. 1895.)

DAUDET, Alphonse *Lettres à un absent*. Paris, 1870–1871. (Lemerre, 1871.)

DU CAMP, Maxime *Les Convulsions de Paris*. 4 tomes. (Hachette. 1878–80.)

DUCROT, General A.-A. *La Défense de Paris (1870–1871)*. 3 tomes. (Dentu. 1875–83.)

——*La Vie militaire du Général Ducrot d'après sa correspondance, (1839–1871)*. Publiée par ses enfants. 2 tomes. (Plon, Nourrit. 1895.)

EDWARDS, H. SUTHERLAND *The Germans in France*. (Stanford. 1874.)

FAVRE, Jules *Gouvernement de la défense nationale*. 3 tomes. (Plon, 1871–5.)

FIDUS (*pseud.*) *La Révolution de Septembre. Paris assiégé.* (Savine. 1889.)

——*L'Essai loyal.* (Savine. 1890.)

——*La Révolution de septembre. La Capitulation – La Commune.* (Savine. 1889.)

FISHER, John *Airlift 1870.* (Parrish, 1965.)

FLAUBERT, Gustave *Correspondance, 1865–1870, 1871–1873.* (Lausanne. Éditions Rencontre. 1965.)

FORBES, Archibald *My Experiences of the War between France and Germany.* 2 vols. (Hurst & Blackett. 1871.)

GAUTIER, Théophile *Tableaux de Siège.* (Charpentier. 1871.)

GIBSON, William *Paris during the Commune, 1871.* (Whittaker. 1872.)

GONCOURT, Edmond et Jules de *Journal. Mémoires de la vie littéraire.* Tomes ix, x. (Monaco. Éditions de l'Imprimerie nationale. 1956.)

GOT, Edmond *Journal, 1822–1901.* Publié par son fils Médéric Got. 2 tomes. (Plon-Nourrit. 1910.)

GROMIER, Marc-Amédée *La Commune. Journal d'un vaincu.* Recueilli et publié par Pierre de Llano. (Victor-Havard. 1892.)

HALÉVY, Ludovic *Notes et Souvenirs. De mai à septembre 1871.* (Boussod, Valadon. 1888.)

HANS, Ludovic *Second Siège de Paris. Le Comité Central et la Commune. Journal anecdotique.* (Lemerre. 1871.)

HANS, Ludovic, et BLANC, J.-J. *Guide à travers les ruines : Paris et ses environs. Avec un plan détaillé.* 3e édition. (Lemerre. 1871.)

HÉRISSON, Le Comte d' *Journal d'un officier d'ordonnance. Juillet 1870–Février 1871.* (Ollendorff. 1885.)

——*Nouvelle journal d'un officier d'ordonnance. La Commune.* (Ollendorff. 1889.)

HEYLLI, Georges d' (ed.) *Journal d'un habitant de Neuilly pendant la Commune.* (Librairie générale. 1871.)

——*Journal du Siège de Paris.* 3 tomes. (Librairie générale. n.d.)

HOFFMAN, Wickham *Camp, Court and Siege.* (N.Y. Harper & Bros. 1877.)

HORNE, Alistair *The Fall of Paris.* (Macmillan. 1965.)

HOUSSAYE, Arsène *Les Confessions : Souvenirs d'un demi-siècle, 1830–1880.* (Dentu. 1885–91.)

HOWARD, Michael *The Franco-Prussian War.* (Hart-Davis. 1961.)

HOZIER, Captain H. M. *The Franco-Prussian War.* Vol. II. (Mackenzie. n.d.)

HUGO, Victor *Choses vues. 1870–1885.* (Gallimard. 1972.)

JOLLIVET, Gaston *Le Siège de Paris et la Commune : Souvenirs inédits.* (*Les Oeuvres Libres.* Février 1928.)

LABOUCHÈRE, Henry : *Diary of the Besieged Resident in Paris.* (Hurst & Blackett. 1871.)

LAFOSSE, H. de *À Bâtons rompus : Tableau de Paris depuis la déclaration de guerre jusqu'à la signature de la paix. 1870–1871.* 2 tomes. (Dupont. 1871.)

LAMAZOU, l'Abbé *The Place Vendôme and La Roquette : The first and last acts of the Commune.* Authorized translation from the French by C. F. Audley. (Burns, Oates. 1872.)

LASALLE, Albert de *La Musique pendant le siège de Paris.* (Lachaud. 1872.)

MALET, Sir Edward *Shifting Scenes.* (Murray. 1901.)

MALLET, François *Les Aéronautes: Les Colombophiles du Siège de Paris*. (Vivien. 1909.)

MENDÈS, Catulle *Les 73 journées de la Commune*. (Lachaud. 1871.)

MICHELL, E. B. *Siege-life in Paris: By one of the besieged*. (Printed by J. Truscott. n.d.)

MOLTKE, Field-Marshal Count Helmuth von *The Franco-German War of 1870–71*. Translation revised by Archibald Forbes. (Osgood, McIlvaine. 1893.)

NEWTON, Lord *Lord Lyons*. A Record of British Diplomacy. 2 vols. (Arnold. 1913.)

OFFICIER D'ÉTAT-MAJOR, Un *Le Siège de Paris illustré – 1870–1871. Le Siège prussien*. (Bibliothèque libérale. 1871.)

OFFICIER DE MARINE, Un *Le Siège de Paris: Journal d'un officier de marine attaché au* ˣˣˣ *secteur*. (Delagrave, 1872.)

OLLIER, E. *Cassell's History of the War between France and Germany, 1870–1871*. 2 vols. (Cassell. 1871–2.)

O'SHEA, John Augustus *An Iron-bound City; or, Five Months of Peril and Privation*. 2 vols. (Ward & Downey. 1886).

OXFORD GRADUATE, An, [i.e. Henry Labouchère] *Inside Paris during the Siege*. (Macmillan. 1871.)

PAU, Jules *La Délivrance de Paris. Récit complet des 8 journées de mai*. (Dentu. 1871.)

POWELL, Dr. O. C. *Reminiscences of La Commune and the Second Siege of Paris*. (Jersey. Printed at the *Chronique de Jersey*, 1914.)

QUÉPAT, Nérée *Simples notes. Prises pendant le siège de Paris*. (Thorin. 1871.)

QUINET, Mme Edgar *Paris. Journal du siège. Précédé d'une préface d'Edgar Quinet*. (Dentu. 1873.)

QUINET, Edgar *Le Siège de Paris et la défense nationale.* (Lacroix, Verboeckhoven. 1871.)

RÉDACTEUR DE L'ÉCHO FRANÇAIS, Un *Le Bombardement de Paris.* (Bruxelles. L'Écho Français. 1871.)

REID, Stuart J. (ed.) *Memoirs of Sir Edward Blount, K.C.B., &c.* (Longmans, Green. 1902.)

RENAN, Ernest *Correspondance, 1846–1871.* (Calmann-Lévy. 1926.)

RICHARDSON, Joanna *Théophile Gautier : his Life and Times.* (Reinhardt. 1958.)

——*Princess Mathilde.* (Weidenfeld & Nicolson. 1969.)

——*Verlaine.* (Weidenfeld & Nicolson. 1971)

ROCHEFORT, Henri *Les Aventures de ma vie.* 5 tomes. (Dupont. 1896.)

ROUVET, Massillon *Viollet-le-Duc et Alphand au siège de Paris.* (Librairies-Imprimeries réunies. n.d.)

RUSSELL, W. H. *My Diary during the last great war.* (Routledge. 1874.)

THIERRY, Édouard *La Comédie-Française pendant les deux sièges (1870–1871). Journal de l'Administrateur-général.* (Tresse & Stock. 1887.)

VALLÈS, Jules *Le Cri du Peuple. Février 1848 à mai 1871.* (Éditeurs français réunis. 1953.)

VANDAM, Albert *An Englishman in Paris.* (Chapman & Hall. 1893.)

VIZETELLY, Ernest A. *My Adventures in the Commune.* (Chatto & Windus. 1914.)

WASHBURNE, E. B. *Recollections of a Minister to France, 1869–1877.* 2 vols. (Sampson Low. 1887.)

WHITEHURST, Felix M. *My Private Diary during the Siege of Paris.* 2 vols. (Tinsley Bros. 1875.)

WILLIAMS, Roger L. *The French Revolution of 1870–1871.* (New York. Norton. 1969.)

Index